THE BEASTS
IN YOUR BRAIN

THE BEASTS IN YOUR BRAIN

Understanding and Living with ANXIETY and DEPRESSION

Katherine Speller

Illustrations by Harshad Marathe

Z ZEST BOOKS
MINNEAPOLIS

**For my brain trust(s) and everyone
who has ever felt like a brain in a jar
—K.S.**

Zest Books™
An imprint of Lerner Publishing Group, Inc.
241 First Avenue North
Minneapolis, MN 55401 USA

For reading levels and more information, look up this title at www.lernerbooks.com.
Visit us at zestbooks.net.

Designed by Viet Chu
Main body text set in Janson Text LT Std.
Typeface provided by Adobe Systems.

Library of Congress Cataloging-in-Publication Data

Names: Speller, Katherine, author.
Title: The beasts in your brain : understanding and living with anxiety and depression / Katherine Speller.
Description: Minneapolis, MN : Zest Books , [2023] | Includes bibliographical references and index. | Audience: Ages 13–18 | Audience: Grades 7–9 | Summary: "A quippy, fun, and empathetic read that reminds readers they are not alone in their feelings, teaches them the science of mental illness, and empowers them to quell the brain beasts of depression and anxiety"— Provided by publisher.
Identifiers: LCCN 2022056809 (print) | LCCN 2022056810 (ebook) | ISBN 9781541599253 (library binding) | ISBN 9781728417202 (paperback) | ISBN 9781728486048 (ebook)
Subjects: LCSH: Anxiety—Juvenile literature. | Depression in children—Juvenile literature.
Classification: LCC BF575.A6 S64 2023 (print) | LCC BF575.A6 (ebook) | DDC 152.4/6—dc23/eng/20230209

LC record available at https://lccn.loc.gov/2022056809
LC ebook record available at https://lccn.loc.gov/2022056810

Manufactured in the United States of America
1-48135-48771-3/2/2023

TABLE OF CONTENTS

INTRODUCTION
Naming That Feeling

I first started writing, reporting, and talking to people for this book in 2019.

And I can't lie to you, writing that feels like a punch line now. I feel as though I've aged a thousand years. My back hurts in places it didn't before. Did all of you get taller?

In 2019 we were *already* experiencing a crisis for young people's mental well-being. It was more than enough for me as a journalist, a formerly mentally ill teen, and a currently mentally ill adult to cover. I'd been talking to middle schoolers, high schoolers, and college students about how their brains were doing (answer: not well!) from my time working at MTV in 2015 all the way to my current work running the health section for a parenting website. So I had an idea to some degree, personally and professionally, that things were not great for teen mental health, and they hadn't been for a long time.

In our world, the struggles in our communities—about race, class, gender, sexuality, fierce social divisions, and general unrest—weigh heavily on the minds of young people facing an uncertain (if not dystopian) economic future, inaction on a worsening climate crisis, painfully frequent mass shootings targeting their peers, and growing up as the first generation raised alongside ever-present technology (that is maybe turning us all into angry cyborgs with an underdeveloped ability to control our rage over a bad tweet and an overdeveloped urge to make content out of everything we post). These and other environmental factors aren't conducive to healthy minds, bodies, and spirits.

So the mental health situation for teens was already a certified bummer. And then 2020 dropped a bomb on everyone: the COVID-19 pandemic. Within a year, the leading experts on child and adolescent health were declaring a national emergency for youth mental health.

American Academy of Pediatrics then president Lee Savio Beers said, "Young people have endured so much throughout this pandemic and while much of the attention is often placed on its physical health consequences, we cannot overlook the escalating mental health crisis facing our patients." She called for lawmakers to take action because "we must treat this mental health crisis like the emergency it is."

Dr. Anisha Patel-Dunn, a practicing psychiatrist and chief medical officer at LifeStance Health, told me in early 2022 that

we've been seeing a significant increase in all mental health issues—and anxiety and depression are just at the forefront. As we think about pandemics or high-intensity situations, historically, I can't overstate how this is just going to be here for a long time, and we really need to give it attention and time and focus. And we need to recognize it's an evolution: That young adults have been really impacted, and this is going to be really long term. Children are resilient, so I don't want to be pessimistic, but I also want to be realistic that this is a crisis that's going to continue well after the physical crisis of the pandemic dissipates.

In 2019 we had no idea what it might mean to embark on these painful pandemic years—of online school, social distancing, masking (or people getting Big Mad about not masking), parents and caregivers losing their jobs, and the everyday challenges of having to consider your health and the health of people you love before taking the "risk" of meeting your friends at a park or going to the grocery store. Nowhere in the studies, interviews, articles, and countless conversations I was having was there a framework for making sense of teens losing parents, grandparents, or even peers to a virus under these complex intersecting conditions. Nowhere was there a perfect, beautiful quote that could comfort you for the very specific ache of missing your senior prom, your last field hockey season, or your big eighth-grade class trip. You felt as though you had no right to be sad because no one you knew had died from COVID-19. Nowhere could you escape the fear and hurt everyone else in the world was feeling since the screens that connected you to all this pain were also your school, your primary source of human interaction outside your household, and often your alarm. Yeah, it's fun out there.

This stuff is impossibly heavy, even for the adults in your

life, to manage. Being a teen under "normal" circumstances is hard enough. Thanks to the fun of puberty, your brains and bodies are Going Through It™ in all kinds of ways that make you feel weird and amazing, bad and good at the same time. The things adults ask of you at school and home are somehow more high-pressure and intense than anything you'll probably deal with in your adult lives (truly, no one is asking us to memorize anything), yet you don't have the same independence that adults do. But then if you add the pandemic, the bad thing that happened to all of us, and all the grief and confusion and unknowns that have come with it, then it's a whole different story. To borrow the word no one ever wants to read again, it's *unprecedented.*

I spoke with many experts about the pandemic, our so-called new normal, and what these might mean for teen brains. One of the best conversations I had, the one that has stayed with me since, was with a doctor who is also a mom to teenagers. She said that one of the best things adults can do to really support the teens in our lives who experienced the pandemic is to release the idea that we can ever truly "understand" what y'all have gone through. Other experts I spoke to echoed this sentiment.

I came to realize that in this once-in-a-generation global tragedy, adults *can* stretch our empathy muscles as hard as they'll go. But we can never truly *be* the fourteen-year-old who had their freshman year of high school via a video call, the college student who left school halfway through their sophomore year expecting only a few weeks of "lockdown," or the high school senior who couldn't celebrate their graduation with friends in person. We know that you're hurting. We can open ourselves up to listen, support, and do our best to help guide you, but the things you've lived through are unique. Your feelings and reactions to them are also unique.

To young people reading this book, you're not being self-centered, dramatic, or blowing things out of proportion when you think "Whoa, this all feels like *a lot*" or when you look at the experiences that have shaped your mental health story with particular sadness. You don't have to fake it and pretend it isn't hard. The pain, confusion, and grief you're living with is all too real.

Although the adults in your life know that things are difficult for you—no matter how much they love you and want to do right by you—they may still be incredibly clumsy, careless, or shortsighted as they try to help you navigate it all. Adults will talk about your becoming resilient, where you learn how to handle the challenging, scary, and sometimes traumatic things that can happen to you. Becoming resilient helps you grow into the person you want to be despite what you've had to live through. We're all going to be trying our best to be resilient, to recover, and to make this world the kind of place where you, as young people, can heal, grow, and go on to have the experiences you deserve too. And we are going to do that together.

Even though I want to understand what young people are going through, I'm not going to pretend that I can ever truly know your stories or feel your feelings—because that wouldn't serve either of us, and no one has time for that. It feels dishonest and hollow to pretend any differently. But I can offer a little bit of what I know from my own story—and all the wisdom a few very smart and compassionate people shared with me—to give you some of the tools to look after your brains during this time and for the unknown and uncertain times ahead. (Don't worry, I'm not going to get into any upsetting details. Here's your first growing-up-mentally-ill pro tip: when explaining yourself to people who aren't your doctors or your parents, personal details don't matter as much as your privacy, comfort, and boundaries. But I'll try to be honest, sincere, and interesting along the way.)

When I was growing up, I lived through my own mental health story that led to my navigating anxiety and depression—battling my brain beasts was a formative experience, something that I can still feel in the person I am moving around through my grown-up life. I can feel thirteen-year-old me when I'm nervously imagining all the ways new people I meet could potentially hate me. I can feel sixteen-year-old me when, experiencing some familiar down moods, I think eating crackers while standing over the counter counts as dinner. And I can always feel the echoes of eighteen-year-old me whenever I call in sick to work because my brain was moving too fast the night before to sleep well and even the thought of conversations or accomplishing tasks makes me tired. But I can also feel her (all the infinite versions of her) when I remember the skills I've had to dust off each time these moods come up, when I remember the conversations I had with my own therapists, and when I reach out to my support system and clarify the things I might need.

Those versions of me always struggled to admit I wasn't doing okay when I wasn't doing okay. I could tell somewhat that I wasn't able to be the kind of "happy" and "good" and "normal" that I imagined my parents and friends wanted me to be (or that I wanted me to be). It felt even worse because I assumed these feelings came naturally to everyone else my age but me. I decided that I must be doing something wrong to feel so overwhelmed, so tired, so very *meh* all the time.

So, unsurprisingly, it took me a long time to find the right words for what I was experiencing: the worry, the stress, the anger, the sadness, and the sinking sense that I was somehow failing at everything before I'd even tried. I used to say I felt like a brain in a jar—detached, floating. Like I didn't belong in my body, in my friend group, in my school, or in my life. And eventually, shut up with these feelings long enough, I was convinced that I was *always* going to feel that way.

Turns out, I was experiencing my first brush with anxiety and depression. And it wouldn't be my last.

I have since learned what my brain was doing in these episodes. I know how the situations I was dealing with at home and school, along with my genetics and brain chemicals working (or maybe not working), together made the ups and downs hit just the wrong way, making my life significantly harder a day, week, or month at a time.

I understand that these feelings weren't brought on by something I did—the chemical and situational combo was a one-two punch: something that's been hanging in my DNA since the start, paired with events I didn't have control over. I know that I can't just will them away with a few good days or positive affirmations (though, don't laugh, I am kind of into those sometimes). I also know that I can't just fake it hard enough to trick other people into thinking I'm fine and that I am not expected to deal with all of these feelings by myself when they kick in. And now, I know a whole lot more about how to look after my brain, how to be kind to myself, and how to appreciate the challenges I've overcome. I've learned how to take pride in the work I've done and feel a whole lot more hopeful about the work I have left to do.

I sure do wish fourteen-year-old me knew I'd someday get to this point and have this perspective. It probably would've helped a bunch.

Realizing at a young age that you're anxious or depressed,

MENTAL HEALTH MIXTAPE VOL. 1:

BRAIN IN A JAR

We're going to be getting into some heavy stuff on our journey together throughout this book, covering all kinds of feelings along the way, so I wanted to make you something extra to help it all go down easier. Playlists and mixtapes are my love language of choice. My friends and I love making them for one another when we're having a rough time. Considering you're here, you're my friend now, and this is your first Mental Health Mixtape for when you're feeling those brain-in-a-jar vibes:

"Vincent"—Don McLean

"Send in the Clowns"—Eleri Ward

"Favor"—Julien Baker

and even getting a diagnosis, can be such a powerful moment. Knowing it isn't just you, that you aren't broken, does wonders for fighting off the meanest voices in your head (hate those guys) that tend to come through in a depressive or anxious episode. It helps you feel less alone, less awkward, and less wrong. But it's not the silver bullet that makes any of it more manageable or closer to going away. It helps to have a name for the ugly, heavy thing curled up on your chest and chipping away at the parts of you that still feel like you. But the power isn't just in naming the beast. I wish it were that easy! That's only step one.

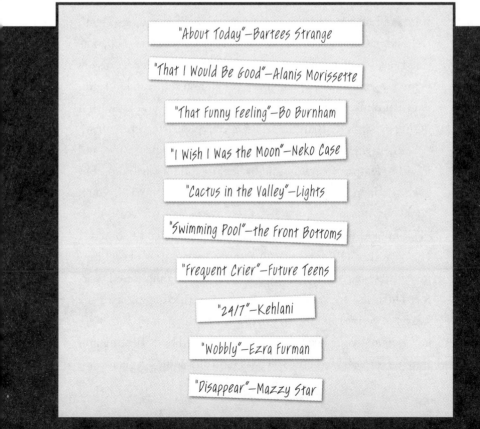

"About Today"—Bartees Strange

"That I Would Be Good"—Alanis Morissette

"That Funny Feeling"—Bo Burnham

"I Wish I Was the Moon"—Neko Case

"Cactus in the Valley"—Lights

"Swimming Pool"—the Front Bottoms

"Frequent Crier"—Future Teens

"24/7"—Kehlani

"Wobbly"—Ezra Furman

"Disappear"—Mazzy Star

For the rest of the battle, you'll need a lot more: You'll need your people. This means the ones who know more than you and me both—doctors, psychiatrists, and trusted adults—and some strategies for treatment (ranging from training your coping skills and talk therapy to medication). You'll need a support system—your family and friends and all the different people who love and care about you (stormy, anxious, beastly parts and all!), who are willing to be honest, supportive, and kind when you can't be those things to yourself. They will also sometimes tell you when you have gone too many days without a shower or eating a vegetable, and you will someday love them for it.

Most of all, you'll need the parts of you, no matter how quiet, tired, and beaten-up they might be, that believe you deserve to feel better, that you deserve to spend days outside your bed, outside the all-consuming brain-in-a-jar feelings. That part of you is my favorite. That part of you is tough and resilient and right. And I promise you, it is so much stronger than you know and definitely stronger than the feelings you're squaring up against.

The fight will look different for you than it did for me, and it will have ups and downs and backward and forward steps, but with the help of the right people, plans, and approach, you'll come out on top.

I hope this book will do this for you: help you or someone you love through naming and taming these kinds of feelings; make these big, intimidating, and sometimes complicated tasks feel a little less so; and get you on a path toward coping with the beasts in your brain and living in spite of them.

Keeping your beautiful brain, heart, and body beating and moving for years to come is what I (and any adult out there who loves you) want to make happen. We want you to live without pain. The world is decidedly better with you in it. You may have an ugly, dirty, and unfair fight with these brain beasts ahead of you, but it's one that we all really need you to win.

CHAPTER 1

When the Brain Beasts Break Loose

For a lot of people, it starts in small ways: You might say no to things more. Hanging out with your friends feels kind of "meh." Projects and hobbies begin to seem as if they'd take way more energy than you could ever muster. You get nervous about going to school—whether there's a particular reason to be—and you try your luck at faking sick a few times or blowing it off entirely just to avoid it.

These feelings might escalate: The mere thought of a test or a big game makes you feel physically unwell. Chest-tightening, heart-pounding *unwell*. Or maybe you can't even begin to care about something that would normally feel important to you— launching a spiral of self-loathing because you can't muster up those caring feelings. Or maybe you just can't get out of bed.

When this worried, stressed, and angry mess of feelings takes over, it can make functioning in your day-to-day life feel downright impossible. How are you supposed to go to school, see friends, and move through the world when *everything feels so intensely bad?* How can you not feel as if you're doing something wrong when everyone else seems to be doing fine—or, at least, better than you? And how did any of these people learn how to feel fine in the first place?

If any of this sounds familiar, you may be dealing with those brain beasts of anxiety or depression. Or even both, since they often hang with each other and feed off each other, like a pair of toxic best friends.

With depression or anxiety, you may be overcome with a feeling of hopelessness or numbness. You probably hear their nasty little voices telling you that you deserve to feel that bad and you will *always* feel that bad.

Those voices? They're dirty liars. These negative, intrusive feelings aren't as impossible to beat as they might seem. But that doesn't mean they aren't big and that they aren't real to you. They *are* big, they *feel* big, and they take up so much space in your heart and mind that I'm sure you wish could be spent on the stuff that matters to you.

But the secret here, something I've learned from years of being a person in a body with a brain that has beasts of its own: Big as they are, *these brain beasts aren't actually bigger than you.* They are only a small part of everything that makes you yourself.

I'll be real with you (I'll try to always be real with you here): These beasts can hurt you in even the best-case scenarios—and at their worst they can be dangerous, terrifying, and disruptive, weighing you down and making you feel alone. They thrive when they get to stay in that dark, unknowable place. They get bigger and stronger when we can't name them, when they make us feel awful enough to stay by ourselves, where they can lounge around our lives, sucking us dry and feeding into that cycle of hurt and pain. They gain their power when we can't even begin to imagine how to live with them, let alone a life without them.

I can't lay out every possible mental health condition and all the technical terms and specifics that come along with them. There's a lot of species of brain beasts out there! But the two common ones we'll be discussing in this book, anxiety and depression, are a good place to start if you're just beginning to understand your mental health journey.

ID-ING ANXIETY

Worry is something that everyone experiences at some point. Like so many behaviors, habits, and features our species has developed through evolution, worry is something our bodies and minds have learned in order to survive. Your ancient ancestors had the sense to be afraid of threatening things (such as big scary fish, big scary things with teeth, and the tar pit), and avoided them to survive. Those survival patterns continued long enough to keep the species going until now. Lucky us.

All that is well and good for our ancestors, but as happens with a lot of things in our bodies and minds that were maybe adapted to help us survive, this feature can quickly become a bug when we're not fleeing predators and are instead, say, trying to send an email. When you can't stop your mind from racing about all the potential negative outcomes you could experience (even and especially if they aren't grounded in reality—like, of course your friends don't secretly hate you), this level of fear and worry can become so unhelpful and overwhelming that it gets in the way of your daily activities and living the life you want. Worry, ultimately, goes away eventually. Anxiety persists.

Anxiety disorders are a medical condition—as real as anything else a doctor might diagnose in your body—that can affect you physically and mentally. The umbrella of anxiety disorders can include a few different things, including generalized anxiety disorder, obsessive-compulsive disorder (OCD), social anxiety disorder, panic disorder, or post-traumatic stress disorder (PTSD). Despite how different these sound, they share some common ground manifesting as intense, persistent, and very often irrational and unfounded fears that disrupt your mental and physical well-being (and your ability to identify, assess and, ultimately, solve problems).

Anxiety disorders are the most common mental health concern in the United States, affecting 7 percent of kids between the ages of three and seventeen and 20 percent of adults, according to the National Alliance on Mental Illness. Most of the forty million adults that report experiencing anxiety say they first developed symptoms of it before they turned twenty-one. These different types of disorders have their own symptoms that can vary from shyness, avoiding certain situations, and agitation to physical reactions such as difficulty breathing, sweating, twitching, or even bowel problems. (It happens! Bodies are weird.)

Some mental and physical signs to look out for are these:

- feelings of apprehension or dread (that raw, stomach-pit feeling)
- feeling tense, irritable, restless, or jumpy
- anticipating the worst, avoidance, or watching for signs of danger
- pounding or racing heart or shortness of breath
- sweating, tremors, bouncing, nervous moves, or twitches
- headaches, fatigue, or insomnia
- upset stomach, frequent urination, or diarrhea

THE DEAL ON DEPRESSION

Although it's far from a fun emotion to feel, sadness is a very normal and universal one. It's going to get you eventually—triggered by a loss, a hurt, a disappointment, or just a few days here and there where you're not particularly capable of being happy for whatever reason. Similar to anxiety's relationship to worry, a period of deep sadness that begins to interfere with your outlook on life and your ability to function daily, and that persists, starts to become more worrisome. That's when you know you might be dealing with depression.

Depression is a condition that often pairs itself with anxiety (toxic best friends, remember?), disrupting your mind and body in similar ways. As the US National Institute of Mental Health describes it, it's a "common but serious mood disorder. It causes severe symptoms that affect how you feel, think, and handle daily activities, such as sleeping, eating, or working." It's characterized by experiencing deep, down moods (sadness, numbness, disinterest, and exhaustion) for periods longer than two weeks.

So it may be that you've been feeling those lows, and that's why you've been choosing more often to curl up on your side and scroll through other people's lives on Instagram or watch some TV show that makes it feel as if your brain turns off. You might see a text from a friend and think, "I don't have it in me to answer right now," and just never get around to it. Or maybe you're tired all the time (either sleeping way too much or experiencing the consequences of not sleeping enough) and the thought of sitting somewhere with your friends, doing that homework assignment, or doing anything, really, makes your brain short-circuit.

Doing, caring, or even wanting to do or care about things feels really hard—as if they're for somebody else, a version of you that used to like things and be fun, not the you that feels as if they're in dimmed-brightness, power-save mode. Not the you that feels so deep-to-the-bone *tired* and *over it*.

These are just some of the ways depression can feel—and sometimes it just feels like *nothing* at all. Like anxiety, depressive disorders come in different forms: major depression, persistent depressive disorder (dysthymia), seasonal affective disorder (SAD), and premenstrual dysphoric disorder are a few examples that young people might encounter. Data from the Anxiety and Depression Association of America estimates that 322 million people worldwide live with depression, and the World Health Organization estimates that globally 1.1 percent of adolescents between the ages of ten and fourteen and 2.8 percent of those between fifteen and nineteen experience depression.

Margaret Wehrenberg is an expert in treating people dealing with anxiety and depression. Since she's written several books and seen countless patients wrestling with these problems, I turned to her to get a better idea of how to identify these feelings in yourself.

"I would say that if you are noticing that you're not having fun when you're with your friends, even if you're acting like it's fun," Wehrenberg says, "if you're noticing that you are having trouble concentrating when doing things you need to get done, those are big adolescent indicators. For some teens, [they] will notice more and more that they want to be getting high or drinking more often than they previously did." She says this may not necessarily be a sign of addiction problems, but people with depression may experience a general feeling that getting high or drinking more would make them feel better.

"And I think another big sign [of depression] is how much they find themselves turning to the smartphone in their hands to get distracted from what they are feeling," adds Wehrenberg.

Depression can present different symptoms, depending on the person. But for most people, depressive disorders disrupt day-to-day functions and rhythms through

- changes in sleep
- changes in appetite
- lack of concentration
- loss of energy
- lack of interest in activities
- hopelessness or guilty thoughts

- changes in movement (less activity or agitation)
- physical aches and pains
- suicidal ideation

OKAY, THAT STUFF SUCKS—WHY DOES THIS HAPPEN?

We're learning more every day about why people develop symptoms of anxiety and depression, and the research shows that the big "why" of it all isn't so simple to answer.

Modern mental health care as a concept is still incredibly young, considering how long we've had brains—it was first mentioned in 1908 by psychiatrists talking about "mental hygiene" and not really mentioned as a field or discipline of study until 1948. While the field has generated a lot of knowledge since then, it also still has a long way to go and more to learn how to provide the most compassionate, affirming, and effective care along with the most effective, evidence-backed answers to that big old "why" question.

We know that depression and anxiety are conditions that humans have lived with for about as long as we've been documenting our minds and bodies. We have documentation dating back to at least the ancient Greeks: the physician Hippocrates (as in the oath that doctors take) used such terms as melancholia, hysteria, and panophobia (the fear of everything) to attempt to describe how people were feeling. Although these feelings have been around for a long time, they haven't always been easy to talk about.

A social stigma (another Greek word!) often surrounds these issues. *Stigma* refers to the attitudes of shame that surround certain people or experiences that tend to pressure people into silence (for example, beliefs that talking about mental health issues should be embarrassing or uncomfortable). Brain beasts *love* when there's a stigma around talking about them because it lets them run wild and protects them from the things that stop them in their tracks (such as your friends, family, and health-care providers).

But that's not to say we're in the dark here. We do know a lot (thanks to wider recognition that mental health is an essential part of your overall health), and health-care providers have become really good at managing mental health conditions.

COOL, COOL—THOSE CAUSES, THOUGH?

To state the obvious, a person might develop depression or anxiety for a few different reasons, and each individual case is just that: an individual case. But the most important thing to remember is that these reasons aren't things you can always control, cause, or simply will away.

GENETICS

You may have run into people in your life (or in your own family) who say that mental health issues "run in their family." As we learn more about how our genes affect our mental health, we also get a better understanding of who is more likely to experience such issues as anxiety or depression. Scientists are even starting to be able to isolate and identify specific genes that they believe might be linked to hereditary anxiety and depression.

As the Anxiety and Depression Association of America says, researchers are "learning that anxiety disorders run in families, and that they have a biological basis, much like allergies or diabetes and other disorders." And some of what they've learned has come in recently.

In 2016 a review found certain genes are connected to generalized anxiety disorder, panic disorder, and SAD, and another review from 2017 concluded generalized anxiety disorder was a "heritable condition with a moderate genetic risk (heritability of approximately 30 percent)."

We're also seeing strides in understanding how depression runs in families. According to Stanford Medicine, "If someone has a parent or sibling with major depression, that person probably has a 2 or 3 times greater risk of developing depression compared with the average person (or around 20–30 percent instead of 10 percent)." They add that people with a family member that had depression more than once or experienced it as a child, teen, or young adult are 4 or 5 times more likely to develop depression than someone who doesn't have that family history.

MEDICAL CAUSES

Sometimes symptoms of mental health conditions can be triggered by other medical conditions too. People with hypothyroidism, Cushing's syndrome, diabetes, HIV/AIDS, and Parkinson's disease, among other conditions, can often experience symptoms of depression or anxiety. Issues with the endocrine and reproductive systems, which manage our bodies' biological processes and hormones (and that are already working in overdrive in teen bodies), are also associated with these symptoms.

ENVIRONMENTAL CAUSES

Our lived experiences can also be part of the equation. Surviving trauma or abuse or witnessing traumatic events (such as the pandemic), especially as kids and teens, can lead to a higher risk of developing anxiety disorders or depression. Stress due to illness or high-pressure life situations such as school, work, relationships, and family issues can also be a cause of depression, anxiety, or both, and so can big life transitions or changes such as a breakup, starting at a new school, dealing with a parents' divorce, or processing a death in your family or community.

Like it or not, the teen brain is kind of in a real tough spot developmentally that makes it more vulnerable to the brain beasts. The 2020 National Survey on Drug Use and Health reported that 17 percent of adolescents surveyed dealt with a major depressive episode in the previous year compared to 8.4 percent of adults experiencing major depressive episodes. The part of our brains that handles things such as emotions, impulsive choices, fears, and reactionary and aggressive behaviors is the amygdala. It develops early in children. But the part of our brain that handles more complex activities such as reasoning and processing our emotions—the frontal cortex—doesn't fully develop until a person is around twenty-five years old. Exposure to drugs and alcohol at younger ages can change or delay the development of the frontal cortex as well.

The reason someone may experience anxiety or depression could be connected to one of these causes. Often, like so much in this world, there are numerous factors that compound the troubles in our minds and bodies—but remember that there's nothing you *did* to bring on your anxiety or depression.

THE CHEMISTRY EXPERIMENT

Brains carry so many wonderful things about you: your memories, your best stories, and your hard-earned lessons. But your brain—like the rest of your body when you're a teenager—is still growing and is, in a way, an ongoing chemistry experiment.

A lot of people in mental health will use the term "chemical imbalance" when they talk about causes of anxiety and depression. This can be a confusing shorthand because these conditions aren't simply caused by your body failing to make "happy chemicals" or overproducing "bummer chemicals." But there *are* naturally occurring chemical messengers, called neurotransmitters, in our brains that can affect your mood and your mental health.

Here's a brief guide to a few of the brain chemicals you might hear about regarding mental health:

- **Serotonin.** This is probably the one you've heard of the most. Serotonin deals with matters of mood regulation, appetite, and circadian rhythms (the biological cycle that regulates when you're asleep or awake). Selective serotonin reuptake inhibitors, or SSRIs, are a common antidepressant medication used to increase serotonin levels in the brain. SSRIs are often paired with additional therapy treatment plans.

- **Dopamine.** Important for memory, learning, and behavior, dopamine is best known as the reward neurotransmitter. The brain releases it when we do something pleasurable. Research has found that diets high in saturated fat can lead to lower dopamine activity, while exercise can help boost it.

- **Epinephrine.** Also known as adrenaline, this neurotransmitter and hormone is tied to the "fight or flight" impulse. It is released when a person gets stressed, scared and, yes, anxious. It can be overproduced when your body is dealing with chronic stress.

- **Gamma-aminobutyric acid.** This is a mood regulator that can help chill out your neurons when they become overexcited. Low levels of these neurotransmitters are linked to anxiety, restlessness, and bad moods.

CHAPTER 2

It's Bad—Now What?

There are a lot of articles, pastel Instagram graphics, and miserable little pamphlets you'll encounter out there about identifying mental illnesses. (Unsurprisingly, I've been handed more than my fair share of these articles, books, and miserable little pamphlets in my day.) You may have made your way to some of the many online resources by doing what feels natural to most of us raised with access to the internet: asking Google a quick, "Hey, wait, what's wrong with me?" For all I know, that's how you found your way to this book.

And we'll all give you the same advice: take the steps to get some help.

I'll be the first to admit that it starts to get a little frustrating—because the sweet, well-meaning and, yes, *true* messages of "Help is out there!" or "It's going to get better" can sometimes sound like nails on a chalkboard when you're in that bad brain space. It's like being told to read an article called "10 Ways to Know You Are in a Gross Garbage Pit o' Garbage" when you're already lying in a bed of rotten banana peels and a rat stole your shoe. Like, thank you, yes, that is established—but how do I get out of here? Navigating all the possible resources available and filtering through all the different voices in this conversation, you sometimes feel as if no one really gets it.

A lot of these materials offer either a generic "talk to a professional" suggestion (good advice but can sometimes be intimidating to execute at first or may not be available to you depending on you or your family's access to health care), some self-care slogan stuff (which is also maybe just trying to sell you expensive leggings), or both. Neither of these answers your "no, literally, help—what am I supposed to do?" questions.

Though drinking water, throwing your phone across the room for a few hours, eating a meal (bonus points for anything with nutritional-ish value), moving your body, and letting the sun touch you for a few hours a day are good things to do and will likely help your mental health, it can feel more than a little insulting to have your existential pain and the all-consuming thing that's hurting you boiled down to "Have you tried turning it on and off again?" Those frustrations are valid, and you're entitled to them. But remember that the brain beasts are intensely invested in having you feel guarded, angry, and dismissive about the techniques that can get them under control.

So no matter how frustrating or impossible it feels, once you have an idea of how to identify what you're feeling, your next step is to get help. I cannot emphasize this enough: Mental illness isn't something you're expected to manage on your own. As the Anxiety and Depression Association of America says, a lot of people with anxiety or depression have a hard time even realizing they have it. So if you've been able to wrangle yourself out from under your own brain beasts to recognize these dumpster feelings, you've done a pretty solid job so far. Seriously, that's a lot!

At this point, you can move in multiple ways toward getting better. A next step might be opening up important conversations with your immediate support system (this could be your parent, a guardian, a trusted adult, or your close friends) about how to relieve some of your stressors and make day-to-day life a bit easier as you take care of yourself. Another next step might be connecting with a health-care provider—such as a licensed therapist, psychiatrist, or even your family doctor to start. If you're experiencing a mental health emergency, you could go for inpatient treatment or the emergency room at your local hospital.

At this stage, give yourself permission to prioritize yourself as you move forward. No matter what plates are spinning—whether school, work, friend drama, or college applications—please know that choosing to put your energy into taming the brain beasts is a good decision. You probably have a lot of other

If you or someone you love is in a mental health emergency—such as experiencing thoughts of self-harm or suicidal ideation, or getting to the point of considering harming themselves—you'll want to seek immediate medical attention by reaching out to the Suicide and Crisis Lifeline at 988 or (800) 273-8255, or by texting HOME to 741741 for the Crisis Text Line. Due to the complicated nature of policing and the statistically higher likelihood that someone in mental distress could be the victim of violence, calling 911 is not always the safest answer in many communities.

high-stakes priorities in your life right now, but you're quite literally not going to be able to deal with any of them if you don't give this care to yourself.

LETTING IT OUT AND LETTING THE RIGHT PEOPLE IN

If you're a young person struggling at this moment, and you haven't already had an adult in your life give you a soft, concerned nudge to check in, or you haven't had a conversation about your mental health with an adult or caregiver, then now's a good time to think about those people who know and care about you and find someone you trust enough to share how you're feeling. This person might be a parent or a guardian, but it's also okay and very common if you are a little hesitant to go to them first.

Andrew Kahn, a pediatric psychologist and neurodivergence expert, says, "For many teens, it may be difficult to talk to their parents . . . as parents are the ones who give or take away their privileges in many households. A [school] counselor is a great first option. Counselors can help [teens] develop the language to talk about emotions and mood concerns, which helps develop a teen's vocabulary about their own life and feelings. Counselors are also trained to assess teens for crisis and have protocols for maintaining safety."

In addition to your parents, caregivers, or older siblings, have "safe adults," as Kahn says, in your circle. Some examples include a family friend, a teacher, guidance counselor, your doctor, a faith leader, a coach, someone at your local

LGBTQ+ center—or a mix of these people in some cases. They will look different in every community, but you'll want each person to be someone you trust, someone who makes you feel seen and safe.

It's also important to note that some people in certain positions, such as social workers, teachers, principals, school personnel, health-care workers, counselors, childcare providers, and law enforcement officers, are considered mandated reporters in most states (and some states place all adults in that category). If they sense a minor is being abused or neglected, they are required to report it to authorities.

Asking an adult to be part of your support system can be an extremely hard, emotionally draining, and vulnerable step. It often involves trying to put your heavy emotions, your complicated concerns, and your needs into clear words—something that even adults struggle with. So be as kind and patient to yourself as you can be. There's no one right or perfect way to do this. Remind yourself again, if you need to, that you are worthy and deserving of feeling good and feeling better.

Once you've tagged in this trustworthy adult, you can start talking about your short- and long-term needs:

- Are you in an immediate crisis, and do you feel safe at home or at school?
- Can any of the causes of what you're going through be addressed by the adults in your community?
- Are there any coping strategies, skills, or exercises you can implement in your day-to-day life to take the pressure off?
- What kind of help do you think you need?

FINDING THE WORDS

One of the hardest things you can experience while navigating your mental health journey is trying to let all the different people in your life know what is going on with you—how comfortable you are with your living situation, your sense of privacy, and the boundaries you have set with your friends and loved ones.

Getting your thoughts together enough to send that email to your teacher or coach or to tell your parents or guardians what you need can feel impossible when you're really struggling. In the following situations, having these prewritten scripts and thought starters can help you get your feelings out there:

Talking to trusted adults about getting additional help and support. "I've been feeling extremely down lately, and I'm starting to worry that something's wrong. I think I need more support and want to look into talking to a therapist."

Experiencing a mental health emergency. "I have had dark, negative thoughts lately that are scaring me, and I am worried that I might hurt myself."

Talking to a teacher about assignments or a coach about missed practices. "I have been dealing with a lot of extra stress lately, and it's beginning to affect my moods at school and home. I'm worried about what it's doing to my mental health. I understand I have [insert obligation or assignment due date here] and wanted to know if there would be any accommodations we could make as I work on these issues. I still care deeply about [this class or obligation] and would appreciate your guidance here."

Talking to friends and loved ones who you've been MIA with or who are hurt by side effects of your depression or anxiety. "I'm sorry I haven't been more present. I have been dealing with some mental health issues lately, and it's made it difficult to focus and reach out to people I care about. I wanted to tell you so you understand it isn't personal and know I care about you. Hopefully, once things start to ease up we'll be able to catch up soon."

Turning down plans because you just don't have the energy. "Thanks for thinking of me! Unfortunately, I am dealing with some personal stuff right now and won't be able to make it. Hopefully, I'll see you soon."

Talking to people who are irrelevant, rude, or low priority (and you want them to leave you alone). "I'm handling some personal matters right now and hope you can respect this boundary I need to set while I do it."

Talking to people who try to make you feel bad about prioritizing your mental health. Sometimes the right response is no response. If someone isn't respectful of a boundary you are setting or is engaging in behavior that tries to make you feel worse for doing the difficult work of taking care of yourself, you do not owe them a response, especially not while you're struggling. You can deprioritize their needs for the time being.

For a lot of people, breaking the seal and beginning to talk about and address these issues can lead them down the path toward recovery—and you'd be surprised how having a few trusted people in your corner can send some brain beasts running. Your trusted adults can help you find peer support and community groups or study up on coping skills that match your needs (you can even find some additional intel on those in the later chapters of this book!).

But not everyone has a trusted adult they can turn to right away, and even the adults who want to help you might not know where to turn. Sometimes we need to call in the pros, and there's no shame in that.

BRINGING IN THE EXPERTS AND GETTING IN THE DOOR

After some talking and opening up, you might decide it's time to seek the help of a mental health professional, if they aren't already looped in. For some people, this will be as simple as asking their parents to set up an appointment with someone and showing up. But that's not everyone's story.

In navigating a privatized health-care system—particularly as a minor—there are some barriers to care that go beyond just "wanting to go" or "not wanting to go" to therapy. Depending on your family's background and finances, there can be other challenges. Your household might be uninsured or under-insured (where the insurance that you do have doesn't cover enough of the costs). Or your family might not affirm who you are (particularly if you're LGBTQ+) or might stigmatize mental health struggles, therapy, and care. If your home life is the biggest barrier and maybe even a contributor to your struggles, your safe adult will be an important resource as you go about problem-solving.

That's not to say it's right, good, or fair that some people will have to do more work to access care. But if we can do anything to connect the dots and make the path to treatment seem a little clearer, we're going to do it. Ultimately, even if you aren't able to get into treatment, that doesn't mean you're without hope or alternatives to continue your brain beast busting. Remember that, please!

WHAT TO KNOW ABOUT MEDICATION IN MENTAL HEALTH TREATMENT

When you team up with a mental health provider, they'll work with you to determine whether medication will be helpful in your treatment plan. As we talked about earlier, our brains and bodies are complex, with a lot of different chemicals working within them—so sometimes, we might need or want a bit of help regulating everything. Health-care providers don't always decide to prescribe medications, but having a doctor-approved medication can help you feel better!

By the numbers, 12.7 percent of people over the age of twelve in the US take antidepressants and 3.4 percent of teens use antidepressants. If you have questions about whether a medication is a good fit for you or concerns about your treatment plan, your doctor will have the answers. I guarantee they would much rather talk about your concerns and share what they know than have you silently worry.

ADDRESSING FINANCIAL BARRIERS

As an American, I can only speak to our specific health-care, uh, *situation*. For any readers operating within a different system, I'm sorry in advance. I wish I didn't have to know about any of this either, and I'll make it up to you someday.

Among American families, Medicaid and the Children's Health Insurance Program (CHIP) cover more than 40 million children under the age of eighteen who qualify for either program. But that doesn't mean everyone is covered: 4.3 million children under the age of nineteen were uninsured in 2020, according to US Census Bureau data gathered in 2021. And numerous Americans are considered underinsured. Mental health experts found in a 2019 survey that 39 percent of people surveyed reported the high costs as the reason they didn't seek treatment. While that was a drop from the 45 percent of people who cited the same reason in 2008, the survey results still show that the gaps in access for low-income and working people are substantial.

Finances remain a significant barrier between people and care, and they can be intimidating to talk about (since there's stigma around being openly low income too). As *Psychology Today* says, the average cost per session for therapy is between $100 and $200—with that varying depending on insurance (with co-pays as low as $10). It's complicated, and you'll understand why adults are feral about insurance all the time.

Regardless of your insurance status, there's often some wiggle room for accessing care when the prices are out of your reach. If you're in middle school, high school, or college, chances are there are some built-in mental health resources in your school. Your school counselor will likely be well-versed enough to help you talk out your feelings, offer coping skills and support, or help you decide what the right next steps are. Many counseling centers on college campuses or in communities have free or reduced-cost treatment available too.

Some health-care providers and offices operate on a sliding scale—they determine the costs based on how much money you have. You can find these by searching "sliding scale therapy" and your area (yes, "sliding scale therapy near me" generally works too). Or, if you're using *Psychology Today*'s Find a Therapist Tool (see page 140), you might be able to determine which providers offer a sliding scale. Sometimes, providers do pro bono cases where that scale can slide to "free" until you're able to contribute.

THE SOCIAL BARRIERS AND KNOWING YOUR RIGHTS

In the best-case scenario, your family shares your goal of getting you help and can assist you as you seek the right options. But we don't always live in the best-case scenario. Let's say that you tried to talk to your parents or guardians and it didn't go well or that your family and home life is one of the environmental factors contributing to your struggles. If you're a minor, these things can create even more challenges in accessing care, but you aren't without options.

DON'T GO IT ALONE
First things first, get in touch with your school or your trusted adult. You can explain your situation to them and see if they

have any suggestions, whether that's coming with you to mediate a conversation with your parents or guardians or exploring alternative options that might be available in your area.

CHECK IN ON YOUR STATE'S CONSENT LAWS

To receive mental health treatment, as with many medical treatments, you (and, more often than not, your parents) must give informed consent. But the age requirements for consenting to care as a minor without your parents vary from state to state. In many states, minors have the explicit right to consent to their own health care—often once they're sixteen and older. But other states have a mixed bag of requirements, and some states won't allow minors to consent without their parents at all. By requiring that your parents or guardians oversee the process, the intention of these laws is to protect you from receiving treatment you didn't agree to. But if you're too young to offer informed consent on your own, they can instead prevent you from receiving treatment you do want.

So fire up Google and check out "mental health consent minor," along with your state's name, for more details. And even if your parents are involved and consenting, if you live in a state where your consent is the only one that matters, you should also know that confidentiality laws apply to you—what you talk about in treatment stays between you and your provider. Knowing about these laws can help clarify your own boundaries with your provider about what they are allowed to share with your parents, and it's not a bad idea to have a fully transparent conversation with your provider about what the state requires them to disclose before you dive into treatment.

AND I HATE HAVING TO SAY THIS: CHECK OTHER LAWS TOO

These aren't words I want to be typing in the 2020s, but here we are: Part of the "fun" of living in "unprecedented" times is watching states enact laws that can have a disastrous impact on already vulnerable people seeking health care. Following the Supreme Court's overturning of *Roe v. Wade*, effectively banning abortions in several states and severely restricting them in others, sexual assault survivors might need to be strategic about the health care they seek and whom they talk to about those choices. Likewise, the increased push for and passing of laws banning and even criminalizing gender-affirming health care can add to the challenges trans and gender-nonconforming people already face in accessing that essential care. The cruelest of these proposed laws also threaten to have child welfare agencies intervene if parents try to help their kids get that affirming care.

While these state-by-state laws can be disheartening to learn about, knowing the law for your area is important for protecting yourself and finding providers who are going to advocate for you.

GO (THOUGHTFULLY) OUTSIDE THE BOX

Talk therapy and psychiatric care may not be essential on your mental health journey. Look online at support groups and organizations (turn to pages 139–140 for a list) to connect with others on similar journeys. You can also look at your local community centers, LGBTQ+ centers, libraries, religious organizations, or state- and local-level chapters of national orgs to see what kind of mental health–centric support groups, programs, or offerings are nearby.

If you find that the thing you need and want most doesn't exist yet, you could absolutely be the one to start one. Obviously, this isn't going to work if you are feeling particularly low or in survival mode, but if you're feeling energized by the idea of creating a positive space for mental health and building one in your community, follow that urge and see where it takes you.

AGING UP AND OUT

Finally, if the health care you need is out of your reach due to your age, please be assured you have all the time in the world to deepen this work once you're legally an adult. If you got this far and know that doing this mental health work is vital and important to you (if so, I'm super grossly proud of you), then you can take steps to work with available resources, such as those discussed in the later chapters of this book, to find support, learn all you can, and try to make the changes you need. It's never too late.

DIFFERENT KINDS OF THERAPY AND TECHNIQUES

You might hear about some of the various therapy and treatment options available to you from your provider or from a thorough hunt on Google. The American Academy of Child and Adolescent Psychiatry commonly recommends these for kids and teens dealing with anxiety and depression:

COGNITIVE BEHAVIOR THERAPY (CBT)

CBT is a common established treatment for young people with anxiety or depression and people of all ages with various mental illnesses. The goal of CBT is to teach you to identify the thought patterns that cause specific feelings (such as the ones contributing to your depression and anxiety) and change those thoughts by understanding them better, using coping skills, and developing problem-solving strategies. Some people say it's training you up to be your own therapist.

DIALECTICAL BEHAVIOR THERAPY

Often used more for older teens and people who might be at higher risk for suicidal ideation and thoughts of self-harm, as well as those with borderline personality disorder, dialectical behavior therapy helps patients accept their emotions and the parts of their lives that play a part in those emotions while also learning to manage and regulate them.

MINDFULNESS-BASED COGNITIVE THERAPY

This form of cognitive therapy uses techniques from mindfulness meditation. It teaches people how to be aware of their thoughts and feelings without judging themselves so that they can better understand their thought patterns and develop more helpful ones.

GROUP THERAPY

This is mostly what it sounds like. Group therapy is a kind of psychotherapy where more than one patient meets with one or more therapists together. It focuses on using group dynamics and the time spent with peers who share similar struggles to help everyone understand their mental illnesses and improve their social skills together.

MINDFULNESS EXERCISES THAT ARE ACTUALLY GAME CHANGERS

If you've looked into getting help for depression or anxiety, you've probably been told to try mindfulness.

Mindfulness is a type of meditation that's about being present in your body and mind, connecting with your senses and your feelings without making a conclusion or a judgment about whatever arises. And even though it sounds a little woo-woo, plenty of research supports mindfulness as a tool not only for people dealing with mental illness but also anyone who wants to maintain and improve their mental health. Some of those benefits include reducing depressive symptoms, such as stress, fear, and rumination (continually focusing on the negative thought), and increasing focus, memory, cognitive flexibility, and self-insight.

Mindfulness has also been found to help soothe the parts of the brain related to depression: the amygdala, the medial prefrontal cortex (which processes information about the self, including worry and rumination), and the hippocampus (which deals with memory and tends to be smaller in people with recurrent depression).

Dr. John W. Denninger, director of genomic research at the Benson-Henry Institute for Mind Body Medicine at Harvard-affiliated Massachusetts General Hospital, says, "Meditation trains the brain to achieve sustained focus, and to return to that focus when negative thinking, emotions, and physical sensations intrude—which happens a lot when you feel stressed and anxious. When you meditate, you are better able to ignore the negative sensations of stress and anxiety, which explains, in part, why stress levels fall when you meditate."

I'm a huge fan of mindfulness. I've found having a more mindful approach to different parts of my life made me like my life a lot more (go figure!), and I've also found a few of the exercises recommended to me help me calm down and pull myself together in high-stress situations. While you should do some research and reading about mindfulness and try different guided meditations to see which exercises work best for you, I wanted to share one of my favorites that's low effort but high benefit:

COFFEE + GRATITUDE

This is my favorite thing to do most mornings when I have the time to be a little slow. It incorporates my favorite ritual, chugging caffeine, to bribe me into doing it. You can use a good cup of tea, orange juice, or water and sit somewhere that's comfortable (it also works if you're waiting for a bus or your ride to school).

1. Sip slowly and consider one thing you're grateful for, with a good belly-filling breath in between sips.
2. The items you list can be small and silly (spotting a particularly chubby squirrel in the fall has made my list) or larger (feeling gratitude for people who make your life better). You just have to mean them.
3. Try to get in touch with how your body is feeling in each moment, and don't let your mind wander. (When in doubt, go back to your breathing to ground you!)

Start with just three breaths, three sips, and three things you're grateful for and check in with how you're feeling—you might enjoy the practice and want to do more!

A lot of therapists use more than one technique or have a preference and background in different ones. If you're ever curious about how they work or why they work, ask your therapist to tell you about them—most therapists are total nerds who love this stuff and would be more than happy to break it all down for you.

THE DOCTOR (OR COUNSELOR OR NURSE PRACTITIONER OR SOCIAL WORKER) IS IN

Let's say, whatever way your story goes, you *have* gotten to where you're preparing to select and set up an appointment with a counselor, therapist, social worker, or psychiatrist.

First of all, please don't panic. For most people, finding a health-care provider who is the right fit for you and your needs doesn't happen immediately. A 2022 survey from LifeStance Health found it takes most young people five therapy sessions before they start to feel comfortable with their therapist. That's at least a month's worth of appointments getting to know each other. There may also be delays between when you first reach out to schedule appointments and when those appointments actually occur.

Patel-Dunn says, "I think what I want to really emphasize here is . . . once you find somebody and you share your story, there's some relief. But it's very anxiety-provoking at first, sharing your intimate thoughts."

Sometimes the nearest provider who fits your budget and is covered by your insurance isn't accepting new patients. Maybe they don't have expertise in what you're going through, such as grief, anxiety, depression, transitional periods, surviving domestic and intimate partner violence, and sexual assault. Maybe their preferred methods don't interest you. Or the two of you just don't click (after all, health-care providers are people, and sometimes people don't get each other). Sometimes someone feels like a total fit on paper but not after a consultation.

Don't be too worried about that. When they first meet a new patient and talk through what the patient needs, most health-care providers are simultaneously thoroughly evaluating and checking in to be sure their style of treatment will help them. The vetting is mutual! Their feelings won't be hurt if you don't connect well enough to work together, and often they can make referrals to local colleagues who might be a better fit.

Patel-Dunn says, "Myself, as a psychiatrist, when I see someone, I can definitely recognize 'OK, actually, I'm going to have you start on medication, but I would like for you to see a therapist' and then can hook you up with therapists because we all have a cohort of clinicians that we refer to and work with. So much of this is just getting connected and sharing your story with a licensed mental health professional."

The most important thing to remember is that taking the steps to talk with someone about your experiences has already put you so much closer toward getting the help that feels right for you.

CHAPTER 3

Troubleshooting Your Support System

Before we get into the nitty-gritty of this chapter, we're going to start with a little exercise. I actually cribbed this from Fred Rogers—the changing-his-sweater-and-shoes guy from the ancient PBS show *Mister Rogers' Neighborhood*— that he did at multiple college commencement addresses and that I've always loved and found comfort in. It's going to be cheesy and gooey, but I swear it'll be worth it.

As Mr. Rogers says, "From the time you were very little, you've had people who have smiled you into smiling, people who have talked you into talking, sung you into singing, loved you into loving." I want you to close your eyes and think about these people in your life, the people you trust most: your go-to friend for a late-night panic-filled phone call, or the person you reach out to when you need to laugh or smile or be on the receiving end of a bone-crushing hug. I want you to think about the small, beautiful, and even weird things you love about them: their goofy smiles, snorty laughs, good advice, and stubborn need to get you to open up or smile when that's the last thing you want to do. Let these people sit in your mind for a bit (set a timer for a minute, I'll wait) and try to intentionally let those memories take up some space. There's plenty of room.

In this chapter, we're going to talk about the part these most important people play in your fight with the brain beasts—and it helps to have a few of these folks you care about at the forefront of your mind as we get started. Because they're solid examples of folks who can fit into your support system. From here, we'll learn how to identify them, how to help them help you, and how valuable they are to improving your mental health.

WHO EXACTLY COUNTS, AND HOW DO I GET THEM ON BOARD?

A support system is exactly what it sounds like: the people in your circle who you can go to when you need help and support.

The University at Buffalo School of Social Work describes the social support system as "a network of people—friends, family, and peers—that we can turn to for emotional and practical support. At school, fellow students, supportive staff, and faculty may provide assistance, and as we move into our professional careers, our colleagues may also be sources of support."

These relationships are the important ones you've been nurturing during your life: your parents, guardians, siblings, and friends. And there's no requirement for how long these relationships have been around. My support system is made up of people who have known me since before I was born, people I met in college, people I met less than a year ago, and people from everywhere in between. It's *never* too late to find your people.

Patel-Dunn says, "Your support system can span friends, schools, teachers, guidance counselors. I think the bigger, the better, in my opinion, because you just never know when someone's having a down day and who can be meaningful."

MENTAL HEALTH MIXTAPE VOL. 2:

IT'S VERY MUCH OKAY TO CRY—IN FACT, I'M DOING IT RIGHT NOW

Guaranteed great vibes for getting a good phlegm-clearing and cathartic cry out of your system. I tested all of these myself. For science.

"Landslide"—Fleetwood Mac

"I Think It's Going to Rain Today" —Nina Simone

"Time"—Tom Waits

"Until I Am Whole" —the Mountain Goats

"To Wish Impossible Things" —the Cure

"The Conversation" —Motion City Soundtrack

"Class of 2013"—Mitski

"The Devil in My Bloodstream" —the Wonder Years

"Feels like Home"—Chantal Kreviazuk

"Fast Car"—Tracy Chapman

"The Story"—Brandi Carlile

They'll be people you trust enough to be honest with about your mental health. They might be the people you open up to—whether it's through venting sessions, pep talks, or crying on one another's shoulders. They might be the folks who are always ready to give you a dose of tough love, the ones who will pull you out of bed, feed you a half-decent meal, and make you wash the sweatshirt you've been wearing for the last week. Or they could be people who help you clean up your messy room, organize your notes ahead of a big test, and help you brainstorm solutions to the overwhelming problems in your life. Sometimes, if they're really close, they can be the people who notice you're having a hard time before you can even put it into words. And they're the people for whom you'd offer the same should they ever need it.

Some people in your life might immediately pop into your mind. But you might be wondering how you can be sure that they are cool with being part of your support system. It's not always a formal thing that you have to say aloud—sometimes it's just an unspoken part of your dynamic. But if you want to be sure, ask. Asking for help or support can be vulnerable and challenging, and so try starting small with someone who already makes you feel safe and cared for (think of your visualization exercise loved ones, for example) by letting them in on what's been going on and telling them what you need. These asks can range from "I've been feeling depressed and might want you to check in this week if you don't hear from me" to "I had a really hard day. Do you have some time where I could vent for a little?" to "Hi, can you please hug me?"

These are the kind of adults you can talk to without being

afraid of being judged or punished. And there may be some crossover with your health-care team and the safe adults we talked about in chapter 2 because they are also a part of your support system! Many therapists and mental health professionals incorporate additional ways of keeping contact (such as texting or chatting by email between sessions) or care plans for when they're not available to help patients who might be struggling or who need support with what they've been working on during their sessions.

A LOVE LETTER TO PEER SUPPORT

In almost every part of your life, you will find people who *get* it. The ones that really understand you and what you're going through when it comes to your mental health. You'll probably find these people among not only your friends but also your peer group more broadly.

Plenty of research shows that people of all ages who have access to the support of their peers—whether it's online or IRL—have better outcomes in reducing depression symptoms alongside traditional interventions. The ability to connect with peers and build support relationships has been shown to "[contribute] to improvements in mental health service responsiveness, safety, effectiveness, efficiency and . . . making services more person-centered," as one study notes. It also allows people to play an active part in their own recovery and the recovery of others, "promoting hope, empowerment, self-efficacy, and expanding social networks."

Teens might find it easier to talk to other young people, particularly if opening up to parents or other adults is intimidating or challenging for them.

Peers looking out for one another is essential—especially for young people who are navigating getting mental health care for the first time, says Seli Fakorzi, a clinician specializing in youth mental health. She is the director of mental health operations at TimelyMD, a virtual health company that provides mental health resources to college campuses around the United States.

"If it's not the student reaching out [to TimelyMD] personally, it's a peer," Fakorzi says. "We're seeing a lot of peers reaching out because they're concerned [about their friends]. But it's been a lifesaving factor for so many students just to say they have a friend concerned about them, a friend that's their age and relates to them on a personal level who urges them to get the support that they need and the care that they need."

Fakorzi has seen instances of friends getting their friends help. Her team had one college freshman who jokingly told her counselor that two close friends "bullied her" into going to therapy. They noticed she was showing signs of being depressed, sat by her side as they helped her get her appointments set up, and talked through her experiences, her symptoms, and the things she wanted to prioritize in her treatment. Was it a challenge for a health-care provider to intake the patient and navigate around a protective group of seventeen- and eighteen-year-olds? Maybe. But were the providers all impressed and inspired by the sheer amount of care and support shown by some teenagers on a dorm room floor? Absolutely.

"Her village and people surrounding her, her peer group, care about her so much that this is the type of *forceful* behavior that they're using to make sure she got the help that she needed," Fakorzi said.

Your village isn't always going to look like people who are sitting next to you, but that doesn't mean you're ever alone. You may find a huge comfort in connecting with other young people online or locally who are also living with and dealing with anxiety and depression.

BUT WHAT DO YOU DO IF THEY DON'T GET IT?

I wanted to cover this section early on because caring for your mental health and trying to heal is a team sport—you cannot be expected to do it alone. But since everyone is on their own journey toward mental health and healing, and everyone has a different perspective on just about everything, getting everyone on the same page (or even in the same book) can be hard. Sometimes people we love or trust are just not prepared for these conversations or have their own complicated relationships to mental health that make them less-than-productive allies in this fight.

Depending on where you live, your background, and how you've grown up, your family and community could have a huge range of attitudes about mental health and mental health care. Based on your experiences, you likely have a very different set of ideas and rules (even if you haven't exactly laid them out) than some of your friends, and you all may have different opinions from your parents or your grandparents. Cultural differences can also play a huge role in how families and various communities approach mental health, with studies showing that such differences can affect how they describe their own symptoms to a health-care provider, the coping mechanisms and strategies they are drawn to, their access to resources, and their trust and belief in whether the health-care system can help them.

Patel-Dunn says,

> I think to teens who struggle with parents not being as active or involved, you can recognize that there are generational differences. Your parents and your grandparents, this just wasn't an open dinner conversation for them. It was just not talked about. Depending on, culturally, where you are from, it's just not something that was accepted or has been accepted. So I think giving it some time and just encouraging young people to be open—it's the same way that I encourage parents to sort of mirror good behavior for their kids. I think we all need to model that for our friends, family, loved ones, for children, and even our elders.

This can mean that someone you care about is unable or unwilling to recognize or get on board with the path you're on. They may say things that are hurtful or dismissive, or they may not be supportive or active in conversations you want to have about mental health.

If someone you care about or trust is dismissive of your feelings, tells you they can't help you or steers you in a direction that feels as if it's not going to address the problem, it is more than okay to go elsewhere. And if you encounter these kinds of responses, remember to *never* feel ashamed for trying to turn to the adults in your community who are supposed to do right by you. Though humans share a lot of the same equipment up in our skulls, we all have so many complicated and different attitudes toward what it means to take care of our minds and toward what getting help can and should look like.

WHAT IF I FEEL WEIRD OR AS IF I'M ASKING FOR TOO MUCH?

This isn't an uncommon feeling, particularly if you're anxious or depressed and have some reservations about asking for help. But honestly, the answer is simple: people want to help.

Patel-Dunn says, "If you're struggling, recognize that many of your parental figures have struggled. Maybe not exactly in the same way, but we've all struggled. So just remember that people really want to help. By nature, we as a society are pretty humanitarian in this way. We do want to help and it's never a bother. No one sees it as a bother."

That last part was something that took me a while to really internalize when I was a teenager living through my own mental health struggles. The brain beasts are generally pretty good at making you feel undeserving of the help and love people are offering—and how can you really accept those good things when you kind of hate yourself? I didn't want to be a bother or a burden, and I struggled to accept that my friends and family

SOME UNHELPFUL THINGS TO NOT SAY TO SOMEONE STRUGGLING WITH THEIR MENTAL HEALTH

One of the less-than-fun side effects of struggling with mental illness among people who are *not necessarily* sharing those struggles is they try to help and sometimes fall short.

Given the full range of different approaches to mental health and well-being, no two depressed or anxious people will always be all right with or offended by the same questions or statements. Everyone's different, so use your best judgment! Here are a few examples that generally aren't as helpful to say to a depressed or anxious person as people might think:

"What do you have to be depressed/anxious about?" That's rude. If the rest of this book hasn't made it apparent, someone could have many things going on that contribute to their depression or anxiety. If you're not close enough for them to confide in you, asking what their struggles are can be extremely intrusive and rude. This can be taken as nosey or dismissive, and implying that they have no right to their emotions or experiences is deeply uncool.

"Have you tried yoga/running/acupuncture?" Although this kind of unsolicited advice often comes from kindness and love, suggesting that someone who is struggling with their emotions, eating meals that consist of no more than crackers, or not brushing their teeth enough needs to simply implement an exercise routine can be dicey—because it can feel to them as if it's just another task thrown on top of an already overwhelming pile of tasks.

You can share something you love that feels restorative and nourishing (like a yoga practice) without being pushy or implying that it will solve their problems—especially if you're talking to a person who has expressed a spiritual or athletic side before.

Particularly if someone is dealing with body issues and you are not their physician, you'll probably want to not offer unsolicited health advice.

"My [cousin/uncle/brother/best friend's dog] was depressed and now he's totally happy." This one isn't inherently awful. Modeling that there's hope and that people have made it through to the other side of mental health crises is not a bad thing in itself. But sometimes, in unsolicited situations, hearing about someone else's triumph while the beast is still kicking your butt can be additional fuel to the self-loathing fire.

"Just be happy" or *"Don't be anxious!"* Again, people who say this usually want to help. They want you to be able to be happy and not anxious, depressed, or both. You probably have that in common. But simply saying "stop feeling that feeling" can be invalidating (again) and maddening—because I guarantee you the depressed or anxious person would simply turn the feeling off if they could. And I wouldn't be here writing this book.

These are also the kind of comments that can make a person who is experiencing mental health troubles turn inward and shut down—rather than affirming or acknowledging their experiences, such comments play into the (incorrect and unhelpful) sense that they simply aren't trying hard enough to feel better.

Pro tip: A lot of these uncomfortable and unhelpful conversations can be avoided if people listen to the person struggling with mental health issues and wait to see if they ask for advice or solutions from another perspective. Listening and providing advice only when prompted has a 100 percent success rate of not weirdly hurting someone's feelings or invalidating them by accident, which is nice.

wanted to give me compassion and care. We'd get into fights about it: they insisted that they want to listen and provide support, and I, doing the brain beasts' work for them, would tell my loved ones to not even bother, that I didn't want them to feel obligated.

But these sorts of relationships, the ones that you nurture with the people in your support system, are tough ones. Those people want to see you come out the other side of this, and they can be just as persistent as any brain beast.

As I got used to letting myself lean on my support system, I was constantly thinking about how I couldn't ever possibly thank or repay them for showing up. And show up, they did—in ways, both big and small, that made it easier for me to focus on getting better.

And many of them were also showing me all the ways I could someday show up for them (and other people I care about) in the future. I realized that the ways my loved ones helped me are the same ways I could help them when they needed it.

Mutual support also feeds back into your relationships, making them stronger, deeper, and sweeter as you all grow together. But remember that this kind of support is not transactional—it's not a thing you need to pay back in exact quantities over time (such as, they listened to you cry three times and now you need to sit through three crying sessions of equal or greater value). And no one person can be anyone else's sole source of support. Relationships don't work that way. But you can begin to learn and understand the ways you can show up for the people in your life as you start to get better (and see how good being supportive can feel).

This can look like matching the energy they gave you when you were struggling, of course, and returning that compassion, patience, and grace if they're ever in a similar situation. But it can also mean spending quality time with a person, showing up for the favors or everyday things that make you a part of their community, and approaching your friendship in a way where you value and honor their personhood, boundaries, and needs in ways that feel right to the two of you. There's no single decidedly "correct" way to do friendship or human connection perfectly (and you shouldn't expect that of yourself or anyone else!). Showing up can simply start with expressing gratitude and saying, "Hey, thank you for being there for me when I was struggling. I appreciate you."

I think humans are at our best when we care for one another. Which brings us back to our little exercise from the start of this chapter. I want you to bring those people and those memories back to your mind. Think of those people in those quiet moments, with gratitude, appreciation, and love. That *is* how you can thank them and repay them. That's the good stuff.

CHAPTER 4

The Dark Place

ontent warning: While much of this book deals with distressing and upsetting topics, this chapter will talk fairly explicitly about suicidal ideation and self-harm in young people. It's upsetting and might be triggering for some readers, so I'd like you to use your best judgment about what will benefit you to read and take in. If you're not ready to read about this just yet, you can catch up with us again on page 80.

If you don't know how you're feeling and if you're uncomfortable reading on, don't hesitate to take a breather, walk around, go drink some water, or talk to someone you care about.

And if you or someone you know is experiencing a mental health emergency or any of the kinds of thoughts discussed in this chapter, reach out for support—either to the people in your life who love you or to professionals who have the tools to help you. We'll have more on this on our resource page (see pages 139–140), but remember that in the US, the Suicide and Crisis Lifeline is a 24/7 service via 988 or (800) 273-8255. You can also use the Crisis Text Line by sending the word HOME to 741741 or via WhatsApp. You are never alone in this, and you really, really matter. The most important thing experts emphasize when talking about suicide is that it is preventable—and these kinds of thoughts can absolutely be overcome, managed, and treated.

That being said, we're going to talk about it, even though it is scary, sad, and hard. Because when it comes to looking out for our mental health, silence is never helpful.

SUICIDE AND SELF-HARM BY THE NUMBERS

Suicide is the third-leading cause of death for people aged twelve to nineteen and the second-leading cause of death for people aged ten to fourteen in the United States, according to the US Centers for Disease Control and Prevention (CDC). Young people aged ten to twenty-four have nearly three times the rates of emergency room visits for self-harm-related injuries than people twenty-five and older, with rates of these cases in girls in 2019 double that of boys, and twice as high as the rates reported twenty years ago. These numbers went up during the pandemic, with emergency room visits for suspected suicide attempts increasing for young people aged twelve to seventeen—a 50.6 percent increase among girls and a 3.7 percent increase among boys.

The CDC also says that suicide attempts are more commonly seen in girls (11 percent) than in boys (6.6 percent), but boys are three to four times more likely to die from these attempts. As data collection has yet to catch up with the realities of how people experience gender, these numbers don't include whether the surveyed teens are cisgender or transgender, nor do they include nonbinary people. Though the data is a bit more limited on transgender and nonbinary youth, a 2019 study from the CDC found that 35 percent of the trans teens they talked to reported attempting suicide in the previous twelve months, and the National Center for Transgender Equality says that "the lifetime prevalence of suicide attempts is 40 percent" for trans adults.

Stats show that roughly 2,877 people in their teens die by suicide each year. One in six high school students have reported that they "seriously considered" suicide, and one in thirteen reported attempting suicide one or more times, according to the Suicide Prevention Resource Center. Teens who identify as lesbian, gay, bisexual, trans, gender-nonconforming, or queer are also more than four times more likely to experience these feelings than their heterosexual peers, the CDC says, with bisexual teens more likely to experience ideation among that group. People from marginalized racial groups (particularly Indigenous people) and individuals with disabilities are more likely to attempt suicide than their white and able-bodied peers—which shows that addressing systemic issues and inequality plays a role in prevention.

These numbers are upsetting, but it's important to know them. These statistics highlight the existence of this huge issue and show us where we can do better. For one thing, the number of suicide attempts remained consistent from the late 1990s to the mid-2010s, but the number of attempts that ended in death increased. This had a lot to do with the methods of self-harm teenagers were choosing:

"Increasing use of highly lethal methods of self-harm presents a significant public health challenge. The reasons teenagers are using more lethal methods to attempt suicide remain unclear," said the researchers. "Some researchers hypothesize that social contagion—more exposure to suicide could induce at-risk individuals to attempt suicide—may be to blame, but there are no definitive answers. More research is needed to understand the underlying factors behind this trend. In the meantime, suicide prevention programs should continue working to address root causes, while also recognizing that the risk of death from a suicide attempt is rising."

The loss of these young people is an immediate and urgent harm, and we must understand this issue with as much compassion, care, and attention as we can.

IDENTIFYING THESE FEELINGS IN TEENS AND WHAT TO DO ABOUT THEM

Being in your teens is an extremely stressful time. Your body and brain are changing, and as you gain more independence, responsibility, and knowledge of the world, it's changing too. These times of transition, paired with the other factors that can cause mental health issues, can lead to some teens experiencing suicidal ideation—having thoughts about wanting to die. There is also passive suicidal ideation, a desire to stop being alive or an indifference to being alive (without making a plan or necessarily intending to follow through with one). Teens with suicidal ideation, when compared to their peers, are more likely to engage in behaviors that could be harmful or lethal to themselves.

These types of feelings can be particularly challenging for young people because, as we've discussed in earlier chapters, their brains are still growing and maturing, and will continue to do so well into early adulthood. With that impulsive and reactionary part of the brain (the amygdala) developing early and the reasoning and emotional processing part (the prefrontal cortex) developing later, teens are more likely to react to emotional issues, despair, or conflict with more extreme, amygdala-driven responses than adults would. This means that it's all the more important that young people have the resources to know what these feelings look like, feel comfortable talking about them, and ask for help from the adults in their communities.

Experts who study suicide and suicidal ideation tend to understand that there's a spectrum in these thoughts and behaviors, ranging from the idea or desire first coming to your head (even as an intrusive thought that you don't actually want) to more passive feelings to the even more dangerous territory of making plans or attempting it.

Signs a young person is at critical risk of suicide, according to the American Foundation for Suicide Prevention, include

- talking about or threatening to harm or kill themself
- trying to access firearms, pills, or other things they can use to harm themselves
- writing about death, dying, or suicide (when such behavior is out of the ordinary)

Signs a young person may be in a suicidal crisis include

- feeling hopeless or deep anxiety
- oversleeping or under sleeping
- expressing they have "no reason" to live, "no sense of purpose," or feel "trapped"
- an increase in the use of drugs or alcohol
- pulling away from their friends, family, and community
- feeling rage, uncontrolled anger, or a desire for "revenge"
- reckless and risky behavior and activities
- significant and dramatic mood changes
- giving things away or seemingly saying goodbye to people

Other situational factors can also put a young person more at risk, according to John Hopkins University Medicine. Suicidal thoughts or behaviors are more likely to happen among teens who

- have experienced mental health issues or substance abuse issues, are living in poverty, or have gone through undesirable life events (such as the death of a parent or abuse)
- have a family history of suicide or violence
- have been in the prison system or have family members who have been imprisoned
- have access to guns or other weapons in the home
- have been exposed to suicidal behavior through their family, peers, or the media

If you or a friend is experiencing any of these feelings, you'll want to immediately get in touch with a trusted adult for help. A variety of factors can cause someone to experience suicidal feelings. Experts emphasize that suicidal ideation is usually related to problems that can be treated—whether that's treating your anxiety and depression (as we've already been talking about) or addressing other issues within your community—and that these crises are very much solvable. Never keep them to yourself or feel shamed into staying silent.

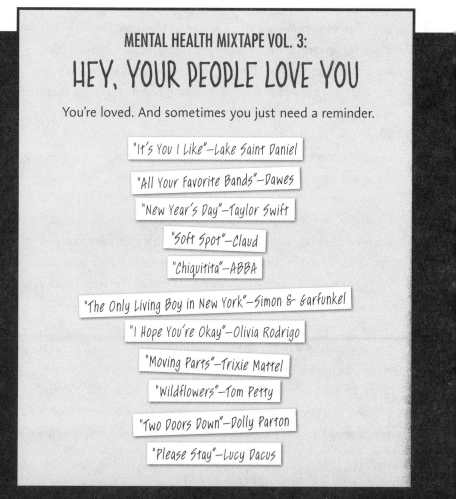

MENTAL HEALTH MIXTAPE VOL. 3:

HEY, YOUR PEOPLE LOVE YOU

You're loved. And sometimes you just need a reminder.

"It's You I Like"—Lake Saint Daniel

"All Your Favorite Bands"—Dawes

"New Year's Day"—Taylor Swift

"Soft Spot"—Claud

"Chiquitita"—ABBA

"The Only Living Boy in New York"—Simon & Garfunkel

"I Hope You're Okay"—Olivia Rodrigo

"Moving Parts"—Trixie Mattel

"Wildflowers"—Tom Petty

"Two Doors Down"—Dolly Parton

"Please Stay"—Lucy Dacus

THE S WORDS: SILENCE AND STIGMA

Many adults avoid talking about suicide, particularly with young people. This silence might come from exactly how horrifying and heartbreaking the idea of losing anyone (a friend, relative, or community member, but *especially* a child or a teen) to this crisis really is for adults in your communities. We want to see you out there thriving, succeeding, and finding joy, whatever that looks like. We get so caught up in our hopes for you that sometimes we don't see your pain, let alone do the more important work of helping you out of it. Combine that with the attitudes some people in older generations have about suicide and the pressure so many young people feel to pretend they are okay or even happy, and you have a perfect storm for silence and stigma, the best friends of brain beasts everywhere.

But experts know that silence isn't the answer.

Patel-Dunn, who has two daughters, said that sometimes these conversations can be as simple as your parents or a trusted adult giving you those crisis line resources. Such an act acknowledges that these feelings might happen, reminds you that lots of people have had them before and overcame them, and conveys that your loved ones want you to feel comfortable coming to them for help.

The various therapists, psychiatrists, and community members I've talked to have all said how important it is that parents and caregivers have these talks with kids and teens—and have them in a way that's vulnerable, open, and clear that the top priority is to get you whatever resources you need to care for your mental health. And it lines up with studies showing stigma reduction (the active work to make these conversations easier to have and more productive) benefits young people by making them more likely to seek the help they need and overcome the silence and shame. Because pretending suicide and suicidal ideation don't exist, quietly hoping they'll never touch you or someone you love, or buying into the myth that bringing them up is going to put the idea in young people's heads, isn't just unhelpful, it's dangerous.

Patel-Dunn says, "We're in a mental health crisis for our children and youth, and suicide rates have gone up. So this is just so critical. People think, 'I'm not going to talk about this with my child because I don't want to give them the idea,' and that's such a misconception. Talking, letting your child know 'Here's what you could do,' or 'I'm here, we can get you help,' and just being open about it [makes a difference]. Let's talk about it with our friends! Let's talk about it with our kids! Let's recognize it's been a difficult time and it's difficult in so many ways."

These dark feelings are scary for everyone involved. But they are even scarier when they're kept quiet and shameful, or when you worry you might get in trouble or cause pain by even saying them aloud. Being open about the reality of these feelings, including the fact that they are completely manageable, not only reduces stigma but also allows young people experiencing suicidal ideation to comfortably seek intervention and treatment options. Some of those include

- **Brief interventions.** If a person is in an immediate crisis, it isn't the best moment to talk through long-term planning and solutions. Odds are, they aren't really in that headspace, and the most immediate concern becomes preventing harm. That's where brief interventions come in. The American Foundation for Suicide Prevention says these interventions are effective for "reducing risk and helping people live through high-risk periods."

- **Safety planning intervention.** This kind of intervention involves working with a health-care provider and your support system to create a plan for how to help you if you experience a crisis. Developed by Barbara Stanley and Gregory Brown, a standard safety planning intervention involves monitoring warning signs; determining activities or locations that can divert attention away from thoughts of self-harm; naming additional people who can help with that distraction, discussion of feelings, and support (as well as professionals available for assistance); emergency contacts on standby (such as the crisis lines at the beginning of this chapter); a plan to reduce access to means of self-harm; and discussion of an individual's hopes for the future and reasons to keep living.

- **Lethal means counseling.** Similar to one of the steps in the safety planning intervention, lethal means counseling prioritizes removing access to methods and means someone can use to hurt themselves in a suicidal crisis. Combining the efforts of an individual and their family, friends, and support system, this intervention acknowledges that you can't possibly predict crises perfectly but that preventing access to means people might use for self-harm greatly reduces the risk of an attempt being lethal.

- **Crisis response planning.** Developed by Craig Bryan and David Rudd, crisis response planning looks at the behaviors, feelings, and lived experiences that led to someone developing suicidal ideation, and then creates a written narrative that explores their risk factors (such as environmental, medical, and genetic) and their specific experiences around ideation. The goal is to come up with warning signs, self-managing and care strategies, support systems, emergency steps, and the many reasons to continue living.

- **Therapy options.** There's some overlap with previous therapy methods discussed on pages 46–47, but a few of the therapy options that are beneficial for people experiencing suicidal feelings are Collaborative Assessment and Management of Suicidality, CBT for suicide prevention, dialectical behavior therapy, attachment-based family therapy, and prolonged grief disorder therapy.

- **Medication.** Your provider, your parents or guardians, and you can also have conversations about how medication might play a role in your treatment. Some common medications considered in these scenarios include lithium carbonate, clozapine, ketamine, and other antidepressants.

ADVICE FOR HELPING SOMEONE WHO IS HURTING

Watching someone you care about struggling with their mental health can be difficult—whether they're experiencing suicidal ideation or something less extreme. We hate to see our friends and family hurt and tend to want to do anything possible to make it better, preferably fast. But, as we've mentioned, the thing with brain beasts is they take a little time to wrangle. At the same time, they thrive when a person is isolated.

If you're on the sideline of the battle, you might feel a bit helpless. You're not sure where to start, and you don't want to say or do the wrong thing and make them feel worse. But the fact that you care about them enough to want to do this kindly and compassionately *is* a good start. Here are a few very simple things you can do to give your loved one what they need while they're struggling:

- **Affirm.** A lot of the most unhelpful and eye-roll-inducing things people can say about another person's mental health come from a place of dismissal or denial. Sometimes just acknowledging that you see them and hear them (and, you know, actually seeing them and hearing them) can be a huge help, and it lets them know that you are a safe person for them to confide in.

- **Ask.** Your loved one is a reluctant expert on how they are feeling. Questions about their experiences can start as small as "What do you need from me right now?" or "Do you want to talk about it?" Depending on the trust and connection you share, you can get into some more frank conversations about the situation or take steps with them to get additional help and support (if that hasn't already happened). These asks can also set you up to really listen, which will help you along the way.

- **Accept.** One of the most meaningful things friends and

family have done for me when I was struggling was to say, "I know you're hurting and having a terrible time. I'm going to be here for you anyway" and spend an afternoon watching movies with me or just sitting in comfortable silence alongside me without necessarily trying to "fix" me. I sometimes call this the Eeyore Rule. Just because you are sad, anxious, or struggling doesn't mean you're not worthy of being loved by your friends. We all have our Eeyore days (weeks, months), and we don't have to spend them alone.

Just knowing that your people see you, understand you, and plan to stick by you through the hard times—even if it takes a little bit longer for you to feel fun again—can be reassuring.

CHAPTER 5

You're Important, So Please Handle You with Care

One of the hardest things but also one of the most important things to do when you're battling a brain beast is to love yourself. When you're experiencing the worst they have to throw at you, you probably don't even *like* yourself that much. That's part of their game.

This is another reason why it's so good to have your people, your support system. They're typically pretty good at doing enough loving and liking to make up the difference while you do the work of getting better. But you should know that you are also one of your own people. And you *need* you too.

So that's why we're going to spend this chapter talking about self-esteem, self-care, and self-love. While your loved ones can take you pretty far in this fight, your ability to support yourself will also come in handy. And you'll find the more you all team up and combine your forces, the easier it all tends to get. Soon you'll remember how easy to like and love you are.

A BIT ABOUT SELF-ESTEEM

The American Psychological Association describes "self-esteem" as the "degree to which the qualities and characteristics contained in one's self-concept are perceived to be positive. It reflects a person's physical self-image, view of [their] accomplishments and capabilities, and values and perceived success in living up to them, as well as the ways in which others view and respond to that person." So, just think of it as how good you feel about yourself—the *real, gooey, and private* inside version of you, not your grades or how many followers you have.

Negative self-esteem can look like being hypercritical of yourself, bad-mouthing yourself, or framing normal parts of life (such as making mistakes or taking more time to learn how to do something new) as epic failures. It can also look like comparing yourself to others, being unwilling to try new things, or having trouble dealing with challenging, upsetting, and frustrating situations that come up.

Low self-esteem works in tandem with brain beasts. According to a study published by the Association for Child and Adolescent Mental Health, "Young people with depression tended to report lower self-esteem than those with anxiety disorders, while those with both anxiety and depression were found to have the lowest self-esteem."

And the National Alliance on Mental Illness backs that up, adding that "low self-esteem tends to work in a vicious cycle with other mental health conditions like depression and anxiety." Often it's not clear which came first or which caused which, but they can hype each other up and make things challenging for you as you start to doubt your value or whether you deserve to feel better.

But self-esteem is something that can be nurtured, boosted, and grown as you grow—particularly when you and your support system work together to build it up. Studies have also shown that therapy techniques such as CBT can help people struggling with low self-esteem.

SELF-CARE ONLINE VS. IRL

The idea of self-care in the 2020s has gotten a little bit twisted. While it might bring to mind some Instagram-friendly skin care montage, a viral TikTok workout, or lighting a fancy candle, its origins go back to both medicine and social activism in the 1950s, '60s, and '70s.

First used by doctors to talk about the things patients can do for their own health that work toward their long- and short-term treatment goals, the term *self-care* was later adopted by academics trying to help people manage stress and avoid burnout from their physically and mentally exhausting jobs. Eventually, the term found its way into the larger political conversations that activists, particularly Black women activists, were having during the civil rights and women's

WHAT IS NEURODIVERGENCE?

You might be tempted to think of some mental health conditions and behaviors as "normal" and others as "abnormal." The brain beasts whispering in your ear might say you should try to just be normal, because for some reason they decided being normal is good and whatever you are is bad. But there is no one definition of "normal," and this unhelpful, black-and-white thinking certainly isn't going to make you feel better. Calling some brains normal can also make people who live with different conditions or whose brains work differently feel ostracized, which isn't the goal when we're trying to understand, grow, and heal ourselves. Instead, there's a better word for these differences in how you think and learn: neurodivergence.

The Cleveland Clinic says, "The term 'neurodivergent' describes people whose brain differences affect how their brain works. That means they have different strengths and challenges from people whose brains don't have those differences. The possible differences include medical disorders, learning disabilities and other conditions."

Not all people who have anxiety and depression count as neurodivergent, but there's frequent overlap and ways in which the umbrella term holds space for all kinds of unique brains.

A few examples of neurodivergence you may already know about are (but are not limited to)

· dyslexia, dyscalculia, dysgraphia, and dyspraxia

· attention deficit disorder (ADD) and attention deficit hyperactivity disorder (ADHD)

· being on the autism spectrum

· bipolar disorder

· OCD

- sensory processing disorder
- PTSD

When your brain, even without any beasts, makes you a little different from your peers, it takes time and reassurance to get comfortable with those differences—particularly when you're navigating systems (such as school or work) that are designed for neurotypical brains. Sometimes you might need extra support, different perspectives (such as preferring visually or auditory learning), or have specific preferences and needs for how to recharge, relax, or function day to day.

Kahn, the neurodivergent expert, says that "neurodivergent teens are most likely affected by periods of feeling unsuccessful or comparing themselves to their 'normal' peers who appear to do things more easily than they do." But he adds that adults and communities can do a lot of things to make sure neurodivergent people are appreciated for their differences and the diversity of their experiences. There's a lot of power in recognizing that the things that are unique to you and your brain *aren't* personal failings—and for many of these differences you can find strengths and empowering parts of yourself that are worthy of being celebrated.

Kahn says, "Teaching neurodivergent teens about their strengths and the areas where their differences can give them unique advantages can help them reshape their identity in a positive way. Additionally, identifying areas of growth for neurodivergent teens can help them develop the skills they need to fit in where they want to, and to show what they know in class or with their peers."

rights movements: How can people fighting against big, challenging, and draining problems (such as inequality) maintain enough energy to keep up the fight? Self-care.

But what does it *actually* look like?

SURPRISING THINGS THAT COUNT AS SELF-CARE

My favorite pandemic TikToks were always the ones where people begrudgingly got themselves up to do the things that they knew would eventually be good for their mental health. Such as taking themselves outside for a "silly little walk" to get some "silly little sun." And I personally endorse doing things that are beneficial to your body and mind, even when it feels inconvenient or like the last thing you want to do, and doing them out of spite. Particularly, when it's to spite a brain beast.

For me, I found once I took those first few tiny steps and accomplished those first few tiny self-care tasks, I became more able and willing to keep going. The small tasks are great because you get all the sense of accomplishment with way less of the work.

I'll give you my own silly little self-love "bare minimum" checklist or inspiration:

- **Go for that silly little walk.** Leave your bed nest, blanket cocoon, or your couch, if that's where you find yourself trapped. Move your legs, then your whole body, and let the fresh air and sunlight touch you. I don't care if it's to the mailbox and back, a lap around your neighborhood, or surprise 5K—it only takes five to ten minutes for it to feel good.

- **Hydrate yourself (and do it again).** Your body is mostly water. If you're neglecting your needs, there's a very good chance you aren't drinking enough also. Sip some. If you haven't had anything resembling a meal today, maybe take a minute to put some food in there too, even if it's just a handful of Cheerios.

- **Do just one hygiene thing.** I have been in the midst of a bout of bad brain days where I've gone a tiny bit too long without a shower, a morning visit with my toothbrush, or a thorough de-yuck-ification of my bedside table— shoutout to executive dysfunction! Choose exactly one of these tasks, whichever feels the most doable, and just bang it out. If you find yourself saying, "Oh, wow, that was not the challenge I thought it was going to be. Why did it take me so long?" try another. If it feels like a lot, take a well-earned rest and know it's awesome that you did the one task.

- **Say just one nice thing about yourself.** This one feels corny and will take a few tries for you to get into the groove of it, but it can help. The nice thing can be really tiny, such as how happy you are that you got up for your silly little walk, how you like your outfit, or how proud you are for doing a lot of hard work to be good to yourself and trying your best.

FILLING YOUR CUP

One of my favorite metaphors for self-care is to imagine it as refilling a cup. If you think of all the things that you do in your life—from school to showing up for your friends and family to any of the hobbies and interests you really love—you can't possibly manage to pour energy into everything if you're too tired, sad, or burned out. Not when your cup's empty! So you have to fill it. Somehow.

This is easier said than done if you're experiencing some of those brain-in-a-jar feelings, that lack of motivation, energy, or desire to do anything—the cup is empty, remember? And being prompted to do things we love can feel like a demand to spill out even more energy that ain't there.

How to fill your own cup depends on what you personally need, but what's awesome is you have countless options. The only rule for self-care is that it has to be the activities that you know are going to benefit your physical and emotional health and not sabotage you further. And remember that the goal is to feel stimulated and engaged, not to try to find the most "productive" form of self-care.

Because I am a writer, musician, and serial hobbyist, my self-care tastes during different stressy and depressy eras of my life always tended toward activities that were a) creative and b) something I could do during the nights I couldn't sleep. I (quietly) taught myself various instruments, learned basic coding for websites, edited long-distance internet friends' boy band fan fiction (a vaguely embarrassing thing to type out), and painted a weird mural on one of the walls of my little basement cave bedroom. These were not pretty, Instagram-friendly forms of self-care I could show off to my friends, but they held my attention, got me talking to new people, and allowed me to make stuff when I was really struggling to remember what it was like to be the version of me who liked those things.

These coping methods and habits followed me into adulthood. When I experienced a particularly nasty depressive episode in 2020, I took up making daily mood boards on Instagram that compiled whatever absurd memes, photos, Microsoft WordArt, or video clips spoke to my vibe for the day—and I was generally upfront, via my "art," about the rounds I was going on with my brain beasts at the time. The mood boards weren't cheerful or beautiful, but they were a low-stakes emotional and creative outlet that helped me feel as though I was taking a few shots at the thing making me miserable. (Pro tip: It's better to aim your rage at the beasts than at yourself!)

This is what I mean by the whole cup-filling racket! Your self-care activity of choice can be as silly, small, and absurd as you like—even if it's just showing off your screenshot folder to a select group of friends and followers who won't ask too many questions.

Self-care can also look like doing the responsible thing. You know, the stuff that your mom and your doctor would give you two big thumbs-up over: putting your phone away before bedtime and really committing to catching z's, making a nutritious meal, or even cleaning your room (I'm sorry, it's true!). Self-care isn't always pretty, easy, or particularly fun in every situation—it's doing right by yourself in the best way you know how. But that doesn't mean that you should avoid your skin care routine, your nice-smelling candles, or some good TikTok-approved dancing. Those activities may very well help you feel a little more in touch with your mind and body.

A LOVE LETTER TO MENTAL HEALTH DAYS

Growing up, I was very lucky that my mom was a true ally to my mental health. Using her own experiences with brain beasts, she let me know early on that how my brain was doing on any given day mattered and that those feelings *did* have an effect on my schoolwork, sports practices, or responsibilities. She introduced me to the mental health day—something I still use.

A mental health day is a day where you disrupt the patterns of your routine, give yourself a break, and do some of the self-care activities that fill your cup back up. A lot of experts agree mental health days can be helpful for managing stress and learning to think of your mental health as just as important as the rest of your health. Beware, of course, of using mental health days as an excuse to *avoid* responsibilities and discomfort—ignoring those problems will often make them worse in the long run.

If you want to ask the adults in your life about taking a mental health day, here are some important things to emphasize:

- **Agree on limits and boundaries.** Unfortunately, no matter how much they love you, the adults in your life are responsible for making sure you're doing the things that are good for you. Work with them to make sure you're on the same page about what a mental health day includes and how often you can use them. Some examples of things you and your caregivers can agree to are no video games or sleeping past ten on these mornings, taking only one mental health day a quarter, or agreeing to extra homework or study time later in the week.

- **Actually do things for your mental health.** You want to make sure you make the most of these days by implementing those good mental health practices we've been talking about. You wouldn't spend a day where you're home with a sore throat or stomachache doing things that make your sore throat or stomachache worse, right? So use this time to prioritize rest, to pay attention to your body and your feelings, and don't underestimate the power of those mundane but good-for-you things. It might be a good day to schedule a therapy appointment or check-in with your mental health provider too.

· **Do things Future You will thank you for.** Consider what you need to relieve some of the stressors in your life: additional studying time (or a clean, organized notebook in legible handwriting), a chance to fully organize your bedroom and make it easier to find what you need in the mornings before school, or a solid eight hours of sleep without a TV on in the background or your phone screen lighting up your face. You probably have some idea of a few things that would make you feel better—more organized, prepared, present, and centered—and I think you will thank yourself for taking the plunge.

And self-care can be found by choosing to be gentle with yourself—especially when things are hard and you're feeling a lot of pressure. (Adults struggle with this too.) It can look like taking a mental health day (see sidebar on pages 90–91), saying no to a plan that is going to leave you worse off, or slowing down when your body tells you to slow down. And it can also just look like being nice to yourself, the same way you'd be nice to your best friend. You absolutely wouldn't look your best friend in the eyes and tell her that her latest math score means she's a failure, right? Instead, you'd probably say something like, "Hey, you did your best," or "I know you're upset, so we're going to do something fun until this doesn't feel so big and bad." Turn these kinds of statements back toward yourself to reframe the situation and be kinder to yourself. Providing yourself the same compassion and understanding that you would a friend is a powerful weapon against those brain beasts, who don't want you to have any kind of positive feedback.

A very cool thing about growing up and getting to know yourself and who you're becoming is discovering all the things that fill your cup. If you listen to your body and check in with yourself as you incorporate self-care into your life, you can learn a lot about the version of you that you like best.

In my case, I always knew playing my guitar was one of my favorite ways to wind down and self-soothe. Sometimes I'd learn a new song, sometimes I'd try to write one, and sometimes I'd just sit and play whatever came to mind. This is still something I'll do when I need to fill my cup. But, as I've gotten older, I also found that more mundane activities, such as making to-do lists for the next few days, making sure my dishes or laundry (or whatever chore I am most likely to procrastinate doing) are done, and doing some goofy stretches when I've been hunched over a computer all day really do the trick. They're not aesthetically pleasing things (except maybe the dishes making my kitchen less ugly), but self-care only has to be for you!

No one expects you to wake up and want to paint a masterpiece or learn the mandolin after being in a blanket cocoon all weekend. But as you make your way to recovery and take up the work of maintaining your mental health, recognizing the things that do add value to your life is a good practice. And when you start to feel as if you have the energy to prioritize nourishing and motivating activities, when you start to notice that happening? That's the cup filling up.

CHAPTER 6

Through the Screens

For a large percentage of young people, it's common to open your eyes each morning and immediately look at your phone. This was a reality prepandemic, and it's even more true in the 2020s when we all regularly woke up to push notifications that could spike even the most mellow person's anxiety. Browsing Instagram, scrolling Twitter, or catching up with texts you might've missed overnight is a natural reaction to being forever on the grid. And since phones are often our first connection with the world outside each day, it became even more of a lifeline, providing nonfamily social interaction while we were in various stages of lockdown.

So even on a good brain day—one where you get out of bed with a bit more of your "youness" intact, where you're excited to see and talk to your friends—chances are, you are immediately opening a small window to all the chaotic and stressful things in the world before you've even left your bed. This small window you carry with you isn't necessarily *always* bad, and there's a lot about it that you really like—the good memes (sometimes ones about mental health struggles that make you feel less alone!), a text pep talk from your best friend, and the many, many pictures of dogs out there, for starters. But it's something that is always there, something that can emphasize your favorite and least favorite things about yourself in the same minute (like taking the best selfie of your life vs. if you've ever accidentally opened your camera to a less-than-flattering angle of your face), something that makes it all too easy to compare your journey with others. It's something that can make you feel so connected but also so overwhelmed, lonely, or both with just a tap of the screen.

And if that sounds heavy, that's because it is. For a person prone to chaotic brain beast-y thinking, all of those things can very quickly turn into spirals about how you're never going to feel attractive, smart, or good enough. Or that all your friends secretly hang out without you or that you can't possibly say the thing you want to say because it'll sound stupid or uncool. Remember, though, that those voices are dirty liars.

Katelyn D., a college student from upstate New York, told me. "I pretty much will check my phone and all social media within five minutes of waking up. It's garbage for my brain, but I can't even help it. It's such a routine at this point. I tell myself I need to check in and just see what my close friends are up to—but it turns into a full-on 'check everything' for the next hour of my life."

I talked to a lot of so-called digital natives—people who grew up in the time after home computers, cell phones, and the internet became widespread and accessible—about how being so perpetually connected makes them feel. And those feelings were consistently mixed.

MENTAL HEALTH MIXTAPE VOL. 4:
AUTHENTIC ANGST
2000s MIDDLE SCHOOLER-STYLE

These are each moderately mortifying and more melodramatic than the last, but I want you to have it.

Here are various mid-aughts bangers that spoke to my own teen brain circa 2005 to 2010.

So, please, rage responsibly.

"The Anthem"—Good Charlotte

"I'm Just a Kid"—Simple Plan

"Everything Is Alright"—Motion City Soundtrack

"Empty Apartment"—Yellowcard

"The Places You Have Come to Fear the Most"—Dashboard Confessional

"Get Busy Living or Get Busy Dying
(Do Your Part to Save the Scene and Stop Going to Shows)"—Fall Out Boy

"Remembering Sunday"—All Time Low

"The Church Channel"—Say Anything Ft. Hayley Williams

"I'm Not Okay (I Promise)"—My Chemical Romance*

* Please listen to the clean version—or at least acknowledge that I told you to listen to the clean version.

For some of them, they weren't even quite sure *why* they would open their phones and scroll. It's not as if they are looking for something in particular, necessarily—sometimes it's just a reflex, a second-nature thing that just happens, a thing you do every couple of minutes or hours. Sometimes, in groups or while alone out in public, it's just to feel less uncomfortable or weird.

For others, even just the thought of red notification bubbles hinting at unread texts or missed notifications can make something in the back of their brains deeply uncomfortable, like an itch that just needs to be scratched. And then there's the same questions that might be racing through your head after any interaction with other people when you're young, self-conscious, and growing: What if I don't know what someone is saying about me? What if I said the wrong thing? What if everyone is having fun without me?

This isn't just a "kids and their phones" generational thing, to be clear. (I'm like this too.) We live in a society that has been super reliant on consistent connection for some time, and that usage has only become more intense. According to a study examining adult smartphone users, 79 percent of them have their phones on them twenty-two hours a day—and 80 percent of them are likely to check their phones within fifteen minutes of first waking up. This behavior is unsurprisingly something experts are also seeing in young people as well, with one 2021 study finding that screen time among American teens doubled during the pandemic—going from an average of 3.9 hours a day to 7.7. Obviously, this increase can be attributed to such things as going to school on a screen, socializing on a screen, and seeking distractions from the increasingly upsetting nature of living through a global pandemic via a screen.

But this is another example of the pandemic exacerbating a behavior that was already proving problematic for young people's brains in the before times. Many teens don't even want to be using screens this much. Dr. Cara Natterson, pediatrician, author, and cofounder of puberty education site OOMLA, says that this increase has led to a shift in young people craving connection beyond a computer and a phone.

Natterson says, "The kids who [were] fully remote at school or on zoom all day, every day have hit a screen limit. They've hit their wall, in terms of screen time, in a way that parents haven't seen before. Kids who are online for classes six to eight hours a day and then for homework another couple of hours a day. They don't want to spend their down time further staring at a screen, although some do. They are fried. They have zoom fatigue like all the rest of us."

But what are we supposed to do about that?

CAN YOU EVER REALLY UNPLUG A "CYBORG" BRAIN?

The classic advice for when this near-constant phone exposure starts to get you down is to unplug. It's often said by someone who did not grow up with a cell phone, computer, or tablet as such an intimate part of their lives, and they make it sound so easy. They will tell you that you need to simply step away from the digital world, that it doesn't matter, that it's not real in there, and that stepping away will make those seemingly all-consuming feelings caused by it disappear. It's like a kinder, more well-intentioned call for you to "go touch grass" (i.e., go outside and get some fresh air), but it often comes from a place of not fully understanding how essential and ever present the virtual world is for young people in the 2020s, the ways online life has informed their identities, and how difficult it can be to separate the physical self and the digital one when it's been a part of you for so long.

The average members of Gen Z (born 1997 to 2009) and Gen Alpha (born after 2010) have few memories of living in homes without the internet. Even if your family is skeptical about technology and didn't give you much free rein with your internet usage, you likely came into your teenage years at a time when Facebook already existed (or was even something that only moms and aunts use). Photos of you as a small child may have been shared online before you could even understand what Instagram was or agree to having your face seen by so many people. There is a nonzero chance your parents or babysitters put an iPad in front of you to distract you on a flight, road trip, or particularly exhausting night. You may have learned to type with greater ease than you learned to write by hand. You probably have friends you have only ever interacted with online, and you may not even know their real names, which doesn't bother you as it might an older person who may think everyone online is out to kidnap you. What feels like a generational divide is a result of technology changing almost too quickly to keep up—so quickly that the adults who invented that technology don't fully know what it's doing to users' brains. But we are starting to get the picture from research on screen time and brain health, with some studies showing that people experience "heightened attention-deficit symptoms, impaired emotional and social intelligence, technology addiction, social isolation, impaired brain development, and disrupted sleep" due to excess screen exposure. And it's okay if you don't always know how you feel about all this.

When I caught up with Dr. Leslie Carr, an expert on trauma, stress, and digital technology, this was where my brain was at: How are we supposed to deal with the sheer volume of *stuff* coming through our phones and computers? And, like, are our brains *okay*?

Carr said, "I'm thinking about some brain research that I'm aware of that has just shown that the mere use of technology, just the amount of time that our brains are spent plugged into digital media, appears to be quite literally changing our brains—in terms of not necessarily their shape, but sort of where blood flows on fMRI [functional magnetic resonance imaging] scans. It's kind of wild data that we are just beginning to fully collect." Carr noted that it's uncharted waters given what our brains were built to do as our species has evolved.

"I think that we're in a really interesting point in human history, where in some ways, we have to be able to live on two channels at the same time," she adds. "It's a relatively new thing that we've had access to this level of information. iPhones and the internet are one thing, but even televisions! My parents were born into a world where they remember getting their first television. It's so new in the scale of human history that our brains have been bombarded with the visual media and this level of news."

While we were talking particularly about news, the idea of living on "two channels" resonates with how young people describe the fake-but-real parts of their off- and online lives—there's an urgency and immediacy to the online part (maybe because it's in your pocket 24/7, maybe because the apps are designed to keep your eyes scrolling and the subsequent ad dollars rolling) that just isn't as present in the offline part.

"There's media that we have access to . . . and then there is what is happening in our immediate surroundings, right?" Carr says. "Even our news system is part of capitalism—which is to say that . . . the news is monetized in such a way that 'if it bleeds, it leads.' [It's] designed to hijack our brains and to get us to pay more attention [to it], because it lights up our amygdala and we get all activated around it in a way that's really unhealthy."

My sisters and I joke sometimes about how our phones have become a synthetic organ. We move with them naturally and reflexively, we store important memories and useful information in them, and we maintain them and care for them just like (if not better than) any other part of our bodies. And the spooky part? We're kind of right. According to humanity and technology experts, our species *are* cyborgs. Like, already, right now. The word is a mix of the terms *cybernetic* and *organism*, a living thing with machine parts. And the role technology, or tech, plays in our lives and societies makes us fit that definition—whether we like it or not, and whether we got the chance to ever really understand and opt in or not.

Prepandemic, tech experts were already discussing us as cyborgs, but probably the nature of the pandemic made it a lot more salient. With Zoom gatherings, parties, and schooling taking the place of in-person contact, and personal conversations, interactions, and experiences happening at lightning speed via Twitter, TikTok, and Instagram, the technological organ became even more essential. But just because young people feel attached to their online lives doesn't mean they aren't aware (and at times even resentful) of how technology and the internet has changed their brains, how they didn't necessarily get to choose that life.

When I'm trying to get the adults in my life who don't regularly interact with teens to understand young people's relationship to technology, I send them video essayist and artist CJ the X's YouTube video "Bo Burnham vs. Jeff Bezos." In it, CJ analyzes the human-cyborg situation and mental health (among other things) through the lens of comedian Bo Burnham's Netflix special *Inside*, which deals with anxiety, depression, and isolation during the pandemic and the dependence on and mixed feelings about technology and the internet.

CJ, as a content creator, knowingly and consensually gives their art, analysis, image, and efforts to a large audience for a living, just as Burnham does. But throughout their essay— which shuffles from rapid-fire jokes, memes, and music theory analysis to sincere calls for young people to take steps to nourish their souls offline—they unpack Burnham's very complicated relationship with Being Online. The comedian has been super open about the ordeal of caring for his mental health and setting boundaries that protect his sense of self as an adult man who was once a viral teenager thrust into the spotlight.

Burnham's experience resonates strongly with the feelings of young people in the 2020s: they were all put in that role of content creator, curator, and consumer before they (and even the adults who developed these tools) could begin to understand what it might mean for their brains long term.

CJ says in the video that "it's almost easier, in a way, when

THERE'S AN APP FOR THAT

With our screens taking up so much of our lives and how we interact with one another or view ourselves, remember there are a few solid ways to use the ever-present technology as tools to care for ourselves.

Here are a few of my favorite apps for you that might be game changers for your mental health:

· **Aloe Bud (Aloebud.com).** A sweet, simple, and surprisingly pretty app, Aloe Bud is your soft reminder to practice some self-care and self-love—whatever that looks like for you. You can set reminders to drink water, take a walk, stretch, or use their in-app journaling prompts—it's a low-pressure way to check-in with yourself on the reg.

· **Calm (Calm.com).** Meditation and mindfulness have been a go-to method for helping people learn coping mechanisms for anxiety, stress, sleep, and mental health struggles. Calm is a great app for folks who enjoy soothing sounds and who could benefit from a bit of quiet time to feel centered. Harry Styles also voices a sleep meditation.

· **Breathwrk (Breathwrk.com).** I am obsessed with my Breathwrk app and keep recommending it to people who find it hard to slow down and give time to themselves during the day. Using science-backed breathing exercises and techniques, the app offers a range of different breaths to help you hype yourself up or calm yourself down. Because it has a bit of a gamelike vibe, you get a nice little zing of feeling accomplished (and, if you're the competitive type, like a winner) when you maintain a streak of good breathing days.

you're a performer professionally. You can call your public activity 'work' and your private activity your 'life.' But most kids automatically plugged into the internet before they had the capacity to speak a grammatically correct sentence don't have any boundary between their time as a performer and their time as an audience member. Performance through social media is so integrated into their existence that they don't see a difference between performing and living most of the time. They've absorbed the anxiety of a performer into every second of their lives."

And when it's not clear where you end and the online performance starts, the connection to that online self can feel even more enormous, all-encompassing, and impossible to disrupt. The need to nurture and care for your physical, mental, and authentic self can so easily get lost. Especially when everything going on around you on a national or even global scale feels intense, scary, and uncertain.

Carr says, "The more present we are with our immediate surroundings, the better our brains appear to function. We're living through a really difficult time where in order to be informed citizens, we need to have some degree of awareness of what's happening in the world outside of us. But there is such a thing as being absolutely too plugged into that because it takes us away from the simple pleasures that exist in the here and the now, you know? A good meal, a hug from someone we love—those things release healthy neural hormones in the brain."

Of course, there are upsides to living in this era and to the information, art, and connection that teens have access to—but like so many things, excess use and a lack of healthy boundaries can do some real damage. Unfortunately, living through "unprecedented times" and our high-stress culture makes it all too easy to get lost in the digital world and miss out on prioritizing a happy and healthy self.

Jelena Kecmanovic, founder and director of Arlington/DC Behavior Therapy Institute told me that "generally speaking, there's definitely both positive and negative effects [to today's technology use]. I think that any of these contentions that [modern technology is] all evil and that the only thing to do is to just cut off young people from it, or enforce some very draconian measures—this 'all or nothing' approach—is really not feasible, and it's not healthy. Like everything else in life, there's a mixture there. At the end of the day, it depends on how we use it, how we approach it."

The internet and the rise of social media has been a fantastic tool for communication and combating isolation—particularly when many people were all literally isolating for years. For folks in marginalized groups or those who might feel different and alone at school or in their communities, it can connect them with other people from all over the world about the things they're passionate about, to share experiences and, often, to feel a little less voiceless and powerless.

Sometimes, you even get an emotional or mental recharge when you look down at your phone and join the group chat, see cute photos of your little cousins on Facebook, zone out scrolling through Instagram, or watch a multihour video essay about a Netflix special from someone who talks too fast. It makes sense that you'd want to enjoy that good, high-quality, and stimulating screen time, particularly if you don't have the option of in-person places to go to connect with others. Your friends are in there! People are making cool things! You feel seen, heard, and understood there!

Kecmanovic says, "If you have a supportive community online—friends on Facebook, friends on Instagram, or Twitter that tend to be in contact, to be supportive and to be understanding and educated about psychological issues—they can be there to provide support. They provide compassion and maybe share something going on in their own lives, and there may be people who recognize when those utterances, or posts, are more serious."

Kecmanovic agrees that "unplugging," while useful in certain contexts and a good step toward wrangling your relationship with technology in your daily life, isn't always effective—especially for people who came of age alongside it.

One of the keys to successfully taking care of your brain while living in a plugged-in world is striking the right balance that gives you the in-person human connections and the healthy habits you need to function—without dismissing or denying the realities of the role being online plays in your life and the occasional happiness you get from it.

A NONDELUSIONAL DIGITAL DETOX

Instead of the "just unplug" approach—which implies that the internet, the screens, and the technology won't be waiting for you when you come back to them—you might want to try a digital detox. The goal of a digital detox is to take control of what role all of this tech gets to play in your life, the value it adds, and the impact it has on you.

As sociologist Michelle Gorea and tech researcher Vincenzo Alaimo wrote for *Psychology Today* in early 2021, "total disconnection" isn't the point of a digital detox. Rather, it's about not passively getting swept up in the everywhere, always-on nature of it. You own the phone, not the other way around.

This kind of detoxing can take a lot of different forms.

It can look like choosing where you want a certain app to live. For example, I have a friend who keeps Instagram off her

SOME NOT-PLUGGED-IN THINGS YOU CAN DO THAT FEEL GOOD

I'm not gonna lie to y'all. Various levels of logging off and unplugging does help when you can manage it. You get a uniquely satisfying feeling when you throw your phone somewhere and head outside, knowing that no one can bother you or otherwise own your time until you decide to pick your phone up again.

And unplugging allows you to consciously and intentionally build up your positive tech habits and boundaries—letting you wield your phone (everything wonderful and stressful about it) on your own terms, while feeling as if it doesn't own you.

Here's an incomplete list of deeply satisfying things to do when you're unplugged:

· Read one of the several books you've been meaning to pick up but haven't had time for.

· Dig your toes into some sand, dirt, or very soft grass ("go touch grass" is a meme and a joke but it's also good for you, sorry).

· Get a cool, embarrassing, or interesting story out of a parent, phone because it made her feel terrible and way more likely to compare herself to her friends and randos she's never met. She only uses it on her computer, which is terrible for sending memes but A+ for her mental health, because it allows her to get what she wants from it without it becoming a distraction or a source of a negative thought spiral. I keep TikTok in a folder in the very back of my phone when I have work to do because this prevents me from getting absorbed by my For You page for hours when I have other stuff to do.

You could set specific times for checking apps and messages

grandparent, or other loved one.

- Watch strangers in a mall food court, a park, or any other public place where it's not creepy to do so. People are fascinating.
- Go pick up some rocks. Maybe throw them, maybe keep them.
- Pet a dog, a cat, or a friendly petting-appropriate critter of your choosing.
- Lay around—outdoors or indoors, follow your bliss!—and think about how your body is doing some supercool stuff such as breathing and processing sensory data (what you see, hear, smell, taste, and feel). Try to feel really present in those five senses for a second and breathe.

on certain nights or establish periods where you aren't going to be on your phone or reachable at all, if that feels good to you. Communicate these boundaries to your friends, and they can help hold you to them. Setting specific times that you'll put down your phone can alleviate stress and anxiety over feeling as if you always need to be super available to everyone. These boundaries can also help curb habits and prevent you from scrolling until you feel miserable. Gorea and Alaimo write, "Getting into a habit of knowing when to put down the device can help teens disconnect from their social media networks and dissociate from behaviors associated with social media anxiety, such as zoned-out scrolling. Down times may be during meals [or] an hour before bedtime."

You might benefit from coming up with rules that feel right to you. For instance, you might decide not to use your phone as your alarm clock. Maybe you'll stay off Twitter or Instagram until after you do something grounding, like stretches, getting some fresh air, journaling, or staring at the ceiling in peaceful meditative silence for a little bit each morning. Maybe texts you receive after eleven at night are just Tomorrow You's problem. Maybe you set specific times each week where you check in with yourself and adjust your rules to your needs. These rules and boundaries don't have to be rigid, since you're growing and changing all the time.

A digital detox can even be deciding you do want to "unplug" from certain behaviors that just don't serve you—for a day, a month, or forever. No one will fault you either way. Just because it's deeply challenging and goes against the norm does not mean you can't do it or won't benefit from it.

The move here, when you're trying to manage those conflicting and complicated internet and technology feelings—and do right by yourself—is to really try to be intentional about the ways you use technology, to take stock of how it affects your moods and your sense of self.

And when you realize you're in the thick of dealing with mental health struggles that your devices make worse, call in support from your family and friends to help you set up these boundaries. This can be as easy as saying, "Hey, I'm

DIGITAL DETOX CHECK-IN QUESTIONS

So you've decided to try a digital detox. Here are a few questions to check in with yourself as you figure out what parts of your daily digital diet work for you and what needs a little bit of wrangling:

- Do you feel as if you have a sense of who you are outside of whatever you're posting online?
- Are the things you share with the internet adding value to your life?
- Do you feel overly anxious before or after posting something?
- Is your phone use messing with your sleep or other parts of your life?
- Does being on [insert app here] make you feel connected to your friends, community, or self?
- Does being on [insert app here] make you feel negatively about your body, your sense of self, or other parts of your life?
- Would you feel better if your phone wasn't next to you right now?

having a rough time and think my online life may be making it worse. If you see me using Instagram or Twitter after a certain time, want to gently remind me that I wanted to step away more?"

Kecmanovic adds that if you already know that you're vulnerable to anxiety or depression, it's all the more important to be extra mindful of the ways you use social media. The upsetting things about being online (your fears about your social interactions or lack thereof, your self-esteem, or your successes and failures) can be made worse real fast.

"Say it's somebody who knows that they are very prone to screwing up their ankle. Because they have weak ankles, they might think twice about going skiing, or if they go, they just have to be extra careful," Kecmanovic says. "It's kind of the same idea. There's no shame in having weaknesses or vulnerabilities. We all have them. But it's important to be able to say, if you have this vulnerability, that you have to be careful about this kind of stuff."

Not sure where to start your detox journey? Here are a few sample ground rules that might be useful for you. Remember, setting boundaries of any kind is a trial and error deal, so don't be too hard on yourself if it takes a few tweaks and adjustments to find your balance.

- **Set times when you're unavailable.** You can use your smartphone to your advantage by using the do-not-disturb function or changing your focus mode to better align with how you want to use your phone each day. Each brand of smartphone will differ in what kinds of settings it offers, so play around and see how you can reduce the number of notifications you receive.

- **Relocate problem apps.** If you know that an early morning doomscroll on Twitter makes your brain hurt, maybe Twitter belongs in a sad little folder at the back of your phone. Likewise with Instagram, TikTok, or any other platform that feels as if it takes more from you than it gives. You don't have to full-on delete (but a trial of that can also be cool!), but put them somewhere that isn't immediately accessible.

- **Set limits on app usage.** Some phones allow you to set timers for specific apps that can help interrupt mindless scrolling and keep track of how much time you spend on your phone. They might take a little getting used to, but some people swear by Offtime, FocusMe, AppBlock, and AppDetox for assistance with slowing their scroll.

- **Try out "office hours" for a week or two.** One common worry about phones is that you're letting people down or missing out on something by not being ready to reply the minute a message arrives. To break yourself from that habit, consider implementing windows where you respond to nonurgent messages (maybe only in the morning or at night) for a few days at a time. This doesn't mean you ignore your mom asking you to pick something up from the store on your way home, but it can help encourage your friends to know that you value them and will answer them, just not within forty-five seconds to a minute of their call.

CHAPTER 7

Who Gets to Feel This Way?

Mental illness doesn't look one way any more than each individual does. A person is bound to react in all kinds of ways when a brain beast goes stomping through their lives, and identity is going to play a part in how they see themselves, ask for help, and work on getting better.

But just because people who take the time to learn about mental health know that's true doesn't necessarily mean the rest of our culture is caught up yet. You only have to look at movies and TV to see a disconnect between how some groups' mental illnesses are viewed compared to those of others—and often some groups of people are just completely erased from the stories we tell one another about mental health and wellness.

Research published in 2022 by the USC Annenberg Inclusion Initiative and the American Foundation for Suicide Prevention broke down how mental illness was represented in the top movies of 2019—with sixty-eight characters with mental illnesses counted.

They found that in the films they examined, 76.5 percent of the mentally ill characters represented in these films were white, 11.8 percent were Black, 5.9 percent were multiracial or biracial, and 1.5 percent (or one character each) were from Asian, Hispanic/Latino, Middle Eastern or North African, or Native Hawaiian/Pacific Islander backgrounds. None of the mentally ill characters were American Indigenous or Alaskan Native. They also found that most of the characters were young people, but only six were actually teenagers.

"Most frequently, characters with a mental health condition were depicted as middle aged (52.9 percent, 40–64 years of age) or young adults (35.7 percent, 21–39 years of age)," said the study. "Only four characters with a mental health condition were shown as teens or 13–20 years of age, three were female and two were White. . . . No children were depicted with a mental health condition across the 100 top films of 2019. However, 16.5 percent of US youth experience a mental health condition—far more than what is seen in films."

As for representation of LGBTQ+ individuals, researchers found that just two gay characters were represented with mental health conditions in 2019 (notably both white gay cis males) and no transgender individuals were represented in these films.

These results are particularly weird because research shows that people from marginalized backgrounds can experience more long-term mental health consequences, can encounter more barriers to treatment and resources, and have stories that are extremely relevant to our cultural conversations and communities.

And that's not even getting into the ways some of these stories do more harm than good for the people they did manage to represent; 63 percent of the films portrayed a character with a mental illness as being violent (a higher percentage than previous years). But the reality is that people who are living with mental illnesses are ten times more likely to be the *victims* of violence than the general population, so misrepresenting mentally ill people as dangerous or to be feared only adds to the stigma that makes people stay silent and not seek the help they need.

The researchers note in the study's conclusion that active intervention is needed to change how mental health is represented on the screen—offering insights on how to change the kinds of stories we're telling (axing stigmatizing, inaccurate, and harmful stereotypes) while busting open the box of whose mental health is worthy of being shared with wider audiences in empathetic, compassionate ways.

"People from all backgrounds can experience negative mental health. Without resorting to stereotypes or tropes, consider how underrepresented characters, those from the LGBTQ+ community, or people with disabilities can be shown with mental health conditions across the life span that reflect the reality in these communities," researchers recommend. "Focus on storytelling that fosters empathy and compassion, and consult individuals from the communities you are portraying on screen to ensure authenticity. Often, well intentioned portrayals can be harmful as experts and those with an understanding of 'effects' research are not consulted. Make sure those scholars and mental health professionals are part of your production and development team."

Of course, media representation is far from the only factor when it comes to how we think, talk, and learn about our mental health, but these on-screen portrayals are a part of how people learn to understand such conditions as depression and anxiety. One 2021 poll asked teens in the UK how they felt about depictions of mental health conditions on TV and film. The poll found that almost 70 percent of them saw the stigma-busting benefits of seeing these stories told in a positive way, and 48 percent said that seeing these stories on TV helped them understand mental health a bit better.

So what effect does it have when these stories only show a few faces that mostly look the same? The already hard work of recognizing your feelings becomes a lot more difficult when you feel as if people who look like you or live the way you do aren't "supposed" to experience mental illness, let alone receive care, compassion, and empathy when they do experience it. When stories play into harmful (and inaccurate) stereotypes out of laziness or for the drama, they send the same messages that the toxic, lying brain beast is constantly whispering into your ear: people aren't going to get it, they're going to be afraid of me, and they aren't going to want to help me or be there for me.

Meanwhile, seeing more realistic, positive, and diverse representations of mental illness and mental health care can also put something genuinely powerful out in the world: hope. A story that shows someone hurting and getting help can resonate with someone who doesn't think they have a way out of the hole they're in. A story about someone who just needed a little more love, compassion, and support; a story that makes you realize that you are not broken or wrong for needing more; and a story with someone who looks like you or your family—these all can reassure you that there is no single type of person who encounters mental illness or who is more or less deserving of affirming, compassionate care than anyone else. Accurate representation reminds us (because we all need the reminder) that mental health care is for everyone.

GETTING THE CARE YOU NEED, NO MATTER WHO YOU ARE

Your identity, your background, and who you are all matter—to you, your family, and everyone who cares about you. So it's understandable if you're anxious about whether your family will accept, affirm, and support all those important parts of you—including your mental health struggles and the care you need for them.

Culturally competent care, as many in the medical justice field call it, can be hugely beneficial to marginalized people—as it's shown to help people bypass the biases (such as racism, sexism, or homophobia) that prevent them from accessing the care they need. Culturally competent providers educate themselves beforehand or come from a similar background as their patients. Then people from marginalized communities don't get stuck explaining a whole part of their culture or identity in exhaustive terms to someone new who might not get how these things interact with mental health. If you're a person of color, an LGBTQ+ person, a disabled person, or a person with a combination of marginalized identities, you might feel more comfortable working with a provider who looks like you, speaks your native language, or is able to show that they have relevant experience to the problems you're going through. As one teen I spoke with, who is on the asexual spectrum (sexual orientations characterized by experiencing little to no sexual attraction), said that finding a provider who understood asexuality helped them unpack their anxieties about being asexual without being told that they just "hadn't met the right person yet" or that "some people are just late bloomers." That said, a lot of providers who come from all kinds of backgrounds have been trained on helping diverse populations and combating implicit biases in their work.

Patel-Dunn agrees and wants to assure you that most mental health clinicians have been doing the work in this space for a long time and tend to understand how to help people from different backgrounds: "We mental health clinicians, we have always been trained on this. I finished my training in the early 2000s, and [culturally competent care] was always part of your training because you really want to make sure that your patients feel comfortable. Being culturally knowledgeable is so important. Oftentimes, people feel more comfortable with someone who looks like them."

If a huge part of your mental health struggles are related to dealing with racism, ableism, homophobia, or any other form of discrimination in your home life or community, ensuring your provider is equipped, informed, and comfortable helping you navigate those issues effectively *just makes sense* and can take some of that anxiety off your plate.

Patel-Dunn also says that if this part of your care is extremely important to you, most clinicians have bios and websites available that allow you to do a little research on who they are and what their specialties are. Not only can you find out if they embrace techniques you're interested in (such as mindfulness, movement, breathwork, or art therapy), but you can also check out the things they have specialized in and a bit about their care philosophy along the way.

I've also found, from helping family and friends find the care teams they need for their mental health, that browsing bios and getting a glimpse at the person you're going to meet and potentially form a care relationship with is a great way to get some of the nerves and worries out of your system. It's not all that different from creeping on someone's Instagram or Twitter, after all. Then a good phone call (either solo or with a trusted adult or friend by your side) can help make sure you're all on the same page and feel comfortable taking the next steps of having a session together.

CONCLUSION

Making Room for Mental Health in the New Normal

We've just about hit the end of our time together. From first accepting, recognizing, and putting to words what you're going through (knowing full well that human bodies and brains are weird, special, and sometimes extremely annoying), to learning to ask for help and build a support system that works for you, to thinking about some of the unique ways— good, bad, and pretty dang complicated—that Gen Z and Gen Alpha's mental health story is going to be different from previous generations, we've covered a lot of ground. I'm hoping you're feeling a bit more informed, a bit more empowered, and even a little bit energized about the ways you can take on the beast that is mental health, in your own brains and in your communities.

So, uh, where to now?

Once you've gotten into the zone, identified what you're feeling, and picked up a few skills along the way that help you keep your own brain beasts under control, you're in a powerful position to share what you've learned with other people. You can even take up the cause, becoming a guide on how we can all make this process easier, more accessible, and just plain *better* for one another and for future generations.

That's one of the biggest, surprisingly optimistic take-aways I got from talking to doctors and young people over the last few years: We are in a prime position to take a good look at everything that has taken a toll on young people's mental health and learn from it. If we do that and do it well, we can use this opportunity to normalize mental health literacy, care, and support, and show everyone how essential all this is.

Patel-Dunn says, "The silver linings of the de-stigmatization of mental illness is what COVID has really brought us, right? Everybody has felt anxious and depressed at one point or another over the pandemic. And so there's a real opening, being accepting and understanding of our own internal psyche and the experience."

Young people are already paving the way for the rest of us. As the American Psychological Association found in their 2019 Stress in America Survey, members of Gen Z were more likely to report getting "treatment or therapy from a mental health professional" than millennials, Gen Xers, and baby boomers. Providers are seeing this trend as well. Seli Fakorzi of TimelyMD was the first to tell me that Gen Z's whole vibe and energy feels disruptive and exciting when it comes to their willingness to seek help and their desire to learn.

"I'm impressed. I'm intrigued. And I think many lives are going to and have been saved because of how much [they] start to learn about themselves," Fakorzi says. "I talk to providers all

NO REALLY, YOU'RE GOING TO BE OKAY

This last one is all about bringing some positivity and celebrating resilience. These are paired best with a good long car ride, a sinus-clearing happy cry, or you and your friends lying in a pile on grass:

"Badlands"—Bruce Springsteen

"Shake It Out"—Florence & the Machine

"The Perfect Space"—the Avett Brothers

"Hold On"—Wilson Phillips

"I'm Still Standing"—Elton John

"Under Pressure"—David Bowie and Queen

"California"—Joni Mitchell

"You Are What You Love"—Jenny Lewis

"This Year"—the Mountain Goats

the time who also have a great deal of respect for this population. They have an idea for how they want to incorporate holistic health and possibly health coaching into their counseling and how that's going to help them in a way that's real. Them understanding what their breaking points are and what their triggers are, and understanding what it means to set boundaries. These are just things that some of our students are learning from TikTok, Google, and YouTube, and I am so impressed."

As I talked to people who have been doing this work for young people for a long time, one thing has consistently shone through in every conversation: there's something special in how teens are moving through the world and in how they are trying to look after their brains.

You're set up with a unique set of challenges—ones none of the adults in your life ever could've predicted or wanted for you—but, as the generation that's the most progressive, diverse, and educated on mental health issues in history, you are also uniquely poised to push our communities forward.

Kahn says,

Real change is possible, but we need to take concrete steps at every level—individual, family, school, community, and beyond—to effectively dismantle the deep-rooted, longstanding stigmas and misinformation. At an individual and family level, we need to not only be aware that mental health challenges and learning and thinking differences are real, but also take action to provide the support that teens need. In schools, we need to encourage administrators and educators to embrace the numerous new ways they assess student learning and performance. It's only when teens—and all people with learning and thinking differences—feel understood, included, and empowered academically, emotionally, and socially will we know attitudes have positively shifted.

Your teenage years are so full of changes—and you happen to be living in a time where the world is changing just as quickly. And probably, if you're reading this, you're one of the many young people who have been touched by anxiety, depression, or another kind of mental illness—and that's yet another change in your life that you've had to be ready for.

But with the tools you have now, you're in a pretty good position to take on the brain beasts that may come your way or the ones that might come for the people you care about. And I promise you, I wasn't wrong when I said they weren't bigger than you.

GLOSSARY

ableism: discriminating against people based on their physical and mental abilities. Uncool behavior.

adrenaline: a hormone released by the adrenal gland when you're stressed that can speed up your heart, blood, and breathing

amygdala: a part of the brain associated with emotional processes

anxiety: a deep feeling of worry or unease that persists beyond what would be considered normal. A nasty brain beast.

attachment-based family therapy: a type of therapy to repair, rebuild, and reinforce positive relationships between a kid and their parent or caregiver

borderline personality disorder: a mental health disorder identified by severe mood swings, distorted self-image, unstable relationships, and impulsiveness

circadian rhythm: a physical, mental, and behavioral process that occurs in a twenty-four-hour cycle

cognitive behavior therapy: a form of therapy based on challenging and reframing behavioral and thinking patterns

comorbidity: a disease or condition that tends to present simultaneously with another

co-pay: a payment made by the insured person to cover part of the bill

cortisol: a steroid hormone produced by the adrenal cortex in the brain

depression: a mental illness defined by persistent and extreme feelings of sadness

dialectical behavior therapy: a kind of therapy that focuses on coping skills, including mindfulness, emotion regulation, and distress tolerance, for accepting negative situations

dopamine: a neurotransmitter connected with pleasure, learning, and motivation

dysphoria: a state of unease, dissatisfaction, or discomfort

epinephrine: adrenaline

hippocampus: part of the brain connected with learning and memory

hormone: a type of chemical messenger in the body that sends signals to different systems and plays a role in growth, metabolism, moods, and more

ketamine: an anesthetic drug used to treat depression in some cases

lithium carbonate: a psychiatric medication frequently used to treat bipolar disorder

Medicaid: an assistance program in the United States to help low-income patients pay for health care

Medicare: a medical insurance program in the United States for people aged sixty-five and older, disabled people, and dialysis patients

melancholia: a defunct term that once referred to major depressive disorder, describing the feelings of intense sadness, loss of interest, and hopelessness

neurodivergence: an umbrella term used to describe people who think or learn differently from what most people consider "normal"

neurotransmitter: a chemical messenger that delivers signals between cells. Examples include acetylcholine, dopamine, gamma-aminobutyric acid, glutamate, histamine, norepinephrine, and serotonin.

prefrontal cortex: the part of the brain connected with controlling attention, impulse inhibition, prospective memory, and cognitive flexibility

rumination: repeatedly and excessively thinking about the same negative event

safety planning intervention: a clinical method for creating a document for how to navigate a suicidal crisis as it happens

selective serotonin reuptake inhibitor (SSRI): an antidepressant that works by blocking the absorption (or reuptake) of serotonin. It is the most prescribed class of antidepressant.

stigma: negative attitudes or associations that cause shame or social punishment

suicidal ideation: a person experiencing thoughts about or making a plan to end their life

SOURCE NOTES

8   "Young people have . . . facing our patients.": "Pediatricians, CAPs, and Children's Hospitals Declare National Emergency," American Academy of Child and Adolescent Psychiatry, October 19, 2021, https://www.aacap.org/aacap/zLatest_News /Pediatricians_CAPs_Childrens_Hospitals_Declare_National _Emergency_Childrens_Mental_Health.aspx.

8–9   "we've been seeing . . . the pandemic dissipates.": Anisha Patel-Dunn, interview with the author, March 23, 2022.

23–24   "common but serious . . . eating, or working.": "Depression," National Institute of Mental Health, accessed November 14, 2022, https://www.nimh.nih.gov/health/topics/depression/.

25   "I would say . . . they previously did.": Margaret Wehrenberg, interview with the author, March 14, 2020.

25   "And I think . . . they are feeling.": Wehrenberg.

28   "learning that anxiety . . . and other disorders.": "What Are Anxiety and Depression?," Anxiety and Depression Association of America, October 25, 2022, https://adaa.org /understanding-anxiety.

28   "heritable condition with . . . approximately 30 percent).": Michael G. Gottschalk and Katharina Domschke, "Genetics of Generalized Anxiety Disorder and Related Traits," *Dialogues in Clinical Neuroscience* 19, no. 2 (June 2017): 159–168, accessed July 21, 2022, https://www.ncbi.nlm.nih .gov/pmc/articles/PMC5573560/.

28   "If someone has . . . of 10 percent).": Douglas F. Levinson and Walter E. Nichols, "Major Depression and Genetics," Stanford Medicine, accessed November 14, 2022, https:// med.stanford.edu/depressiongenetics/mddandgenes.html.

36   "For many teens . . . for maintaining safety.": Andrew Kahn, email interview with the author, March 30, 2022.

36   "safe adults": Kahn.

48   "Meditation trains the . . . when you meditate.": "How Meditation Helps with Depression," Harvard Health Publishing, accessed February 12, 2021, https://www.health .harvard.edu/mind-and-mood/how-meditation-helps-with -depression.

50   "I think what . . . your intimate thoughts.": Patel-Dunn, interview.

51   "Myself, as a . . . mental health professional.": Patel-Dunn.

53   "From the time . . . you into loving.": Fred Rogers, *Won't You Be My Neighbor?*, directed by Morgan Neville (Universal City, CA: Focus Features, 2018).

54   "a network of . . . sources of support.": "Developing Your Support System," University at Buffalo School of Social Work, accessed July 2022, https://socialwork.buffalo.edu /resources/self-care-starter-kit/additional-self-care-resources /developing-your-support-system.html.

55   "Your support system . . . can be meaningful.": Patel-Dunn, interview.

57   "[contribute] to improvements . . . expanding social networks.": Bernd Puschner et al., "Using Peer Support in Developing Empowering Mental Health Services (UPSIDES): Background, Rationale and Methodology," *Annals of Global Health* 85, no. 1 (April 2019): 53, https:// www.ncbi.nlm.nih.gov/pmc/articles/PMC6634474/.

58   "If it's not . . . that they need.": Seli Fakorzi, interview with the author, March 29, 2022.

58   "bullied her": Fakorzi.

59   "Her village and . . . that she needed.": Fakorzi.

60   "I think to . . . even our elders.": Patel-Dunn, interview.

61   "If you're struggling . . . as a bother.": Patel-Dunn.

69   "the lifetime prevalence . . . is 40 percent": Sandy E. James et al., *2015 U.S. Transgender Survey (USTS)*, Inter-university Consortium for Political and Social Research, May 22, 2019, https://doi.org/10.3886/ICPSR37229.v1.

69   "seriously considered": "Preventing Suicide: The Role of High School Mental Health Providers," Suicide Prevention Resource Center, May 2019, https://sprc.org/sites/default /files/resource-program/Role%20of%20HS%20MH %20Providers%209_22.pdf.

70   "Increasing use of . . . attempt is rising.": Alicia VanOrman and Beth Jarosz, "Suicide Replaces Homicide as Second-Leading Cause of Death among U.S. Teenagers," Population Reference Bureau, June 9, 2016, accessed November 2, 2022, https://www.prb.org/resources/suicide-replaces-homicide-as -second-leading-cause-of-death-among-u-s-teenagers/.

75   "We're in a . . . so many ways.": Patel-Dunn, interview.

76 "Brief Interventions for Managing Suicidal Crises," American Foundation for Suicide Prevention, accessed November 14, 2022, https://afsp.org/brief-interventions-for-managing-suicidal-crises.

82 "degree to which . . . to that person.": *APA Dictionary of Psychology*, American Psychological Association, s.v. "self-esteem (n.)," accessed February 15, 2021, https://dictionary.apa.org/self-esteem.

82 "Young people with . . . the lowest self-esteem.": Melanie Fennell and Maria Loades, "The Overlap between Low Self-Esteem and Anxiety/Depression in CAMHS," Association for Child and Adolescent Mental Health, January 10, 2022, https://www.acamh.org/research-digest/self-esteem-anxiety-depression/.

83 "low self-esteem tends . . . depression and anxiety.": Anne Gold, "Why Self-Esteem Is Important for Mental Health," National Alliance on Mental Illness, July 12, 2016, https://www.nami.org/Blogs/NAMI-Blog/July-2016/Why-Self-Esteem-Is-Important-for-Mental-Health.

84 "The term 'neurodivergent' . . . and other conditions.": "Neurodivergent: What It Is, Symptoms & Types," Cleveland Clinic, June 2, 2022, https://my.clevelandclinic.org/health/symptoms/23154-neurodivergent.

85 "neurodivergent teens are . . . than they do.": Kahn, interview.

85 "Teaching neurodivergent teens . . . with their peers.": Kahn.

96 "I pretty much . . . of my life.": Katelyn D., interview with the author, September 17, 2019.

99 "The kids who . . . rest of us.": Cara Natterson, interview with the author, February 1, 2020.

100–101 "heightened attention-deficit symptoms . . . and disrupted sleep": "Brain Health Consequences of Digital Technology Use," NCBI, accessed July 21, 2022, https://www.ncbi.nlm.nih.gov/pmc/articles/PMC7366948.

101 "I'm thinking about . . . to fully collect.": Leslie Carr, interview with the author, May 25, 2022.

101 "I think that . . . level of news.": Carr.

102 "There's media that . . . that's really unhealthy.": Carr.

103, 105 "it's almost easier . . . of their lives.": "Bo Burnham vs. Jeff Bezos," YouTube video, 01:18:04, posted by CJ the X,

August 20, 2021, https://www.youtube.com/watch?v
=UvYcunuF3Eo.

105   "The more present . . . in the brain.": Carr, interview.

106   "generally speaking, there's . . . we approach it.": Jelena
Kecmanovic, interview with the author, August 31, 2019.

107   "If you have . . . are more serious." Kecmanovic.

108   "total disconnection": Michelle Gorea and Vincenzo Alaimo,
"Teens and Technology: A Guide to Digital 'Detoxing,'"
Psychology Today, May 1, 2021, https://www.psychologytoday
.com/us/blog/being-your-selfie/202105/teens-and-technology
-guide-digital-detoxing.

110   "Getting into a . . . hour before bedtime.": Gorea and Alaimo.

112   "Say it's somebody . . . kind of stuff.": Kecmanovic, interview.

116   "Most frequently, characters . . . seen in films.": Stacey L.
Smith, "Mental Health Conditions across 200 Popular Films:
A Research Update from 2016 to 2019," USC Annenberg
Inclusion Initiative, May 5, 2022, https://assets.uscannenberg
.org/docs/aii-mental-health-2022-05-02.pdf.

117   "People from all . . . and development team.": Smith.

120   "We mental health . . . looks like them.": Patel-Dunn,
interview.

123   "The silver linings . . . and the experience.": Patel-Dunn.

123   "treatment or therapy . . . mental health professional": Sophie
Bethune, "Gen Z More Likely to Report Mental Health
Concerns," *Monitor on Psychology* 50, no. 1 (January 2019),
https://www.apa.org/monitor/2019/01/gen-z.

124–125   "I'm impressed. I'm . . . am so impressed.": Fakorzi, interview.

125–126   "Real change is . . . have positively shifted.": Kahn, interview.

SELECTED BIBLIOGRAPHY

"Adolescent Mental Health." World Health Organization, November 17, 2021. https://www.who.int/news-room/fact-sheets/detail/adolescent -mental-health.

Anderson, Monica, and Jingjing Jiang. "Teens, Social Media and Technology 2018." Pew Research Center, May 31, 2018. https://www.pewresearch .org/internet/2018/05/31/teens-social-media-technology-2018/.

"Anxiety Disorders." National Alliance on Mental Illness, December 2017. https://www.nami.org/About-Mental-Illness/Mental-Health-Conditions /Anxiety-Disorders.

"Are Our Devices Turning Us into a New Kind of Human?" NPR, September 11, 2015. https://www.npr.org/transcripts/438944317.

Boonstra, Heather D., and Elizabeth Nash. "Minors and the Right to Consent to Health Care." *Guttmacher Policy Review* 3, no. 4 (August 1, 2000). https://www.guttmacher.org/gpr/2000/08/minors-and-right-consent -health-care.

Brogan, Jan. "Teens' Brains Make Them More Vulnerable to Suicide." *Boston Globe*, March 9, 2014. https://www.bostonglobe.com/lifestyle/health -wellness/2014/03/09/brain-development-makes-teens-more-vulnerable -suicide-and-mood-disorders/tGBStHOnjqAyanfCe7rbsK/story.html.

Bryan, Craig J. "About the Crisis Response Plan." Crisis Response Planning for Suicide Prevention. Accessed November 14, 2022. https:// crpforsuicide.com/about.

Bunch, Lisa N., and Amogh U. Bandekar. "Uninsured Rates for Children in Poverty Increased 2018–2020." US Census Bureau, September 14, 2021. https://www.census.gov/library/stories/2021/09/uninsured-rates-for -children-in-poverty-increased-2018-2020.html.

Conron, Kerith J., and Kathryn O'Neill. "Prohibiting Gender-Affirming Medical Care for Youth." UCLA School of Law Williams Institute. Accessed July 21, 2022. https://williamsinstitute.law.ucla.edu/wp-content /uploads/Trans-Youth-Health-Bans-Feb-2020.pdf.

Conroy, Jessica, Luona Lin, and Amrita Ghaness. "Why People Aren't Getting the Care They Need." *Monitor on Psychology* 51, no. 5 (July 2020): 21. https://www.apa.org/monitor/2020/07/datapoint-care.

Crane, Rebecca. *Mindfulness-Based Cognitive Therapy.* 2nd ed. New York: Routledge, 2017. https://doi.org/10.4324/9781315627229.

Crocq, Marc-Antoine. "A History of Anxiety: From Hippocrates to DSM." *Dialogues in Clinical Neuroscience* 17, no. 3 (September 2015): 319–325. https://doi.org/10.31887/DCNS.2015.17.3/macrocq.

"Culture Counts: The Influence of Culture and Society on Mental Health." In *Mental Health: Culture, Race, and Ethnicity: A Supplement to Mental Health: A Report of the Surgeon General.* Rockville, MD: United States Substance Abuse and Mental Health Services Administration, 2001. https://www.ncbi .nlm.nih.gov/books/NBK44249/.

Davis, Daphne M., and Jeffrey A. Hayes. "What Are the Benefits of Mindfulness?" *Monitor on Psychology* 43, no. 7 (July/August 2012): 64. https://www.apa.org/monitor/2012/07-08/ce-corner/.

Dawson, Lindsey, Jennifer Kates, and MaryBeth Musumeci. "Youth Access to Gender Affirming Care: The Federal and State Policy Landscape." KFF, June 1, 2022. https://www.kff.org/other/issue-brief/youth-access-to-gender -affirming-care-the-federal-and-state-policy-landscape/.

"Disparities in Suicide." Centers for Disease Control and Prevention. Accessed March 29, 2022. https://www.cdc.gov/suicide/facts/disparities -in-suicide.html.

Gottschalk, Michael G., and Katharina Domschke. "Novel Developments in Genetic and Epigenetic Mechanisms of Anxiety." *Current Opinion in Psychiatry* 29, no. 1 (January 2016): 32–38. https://doi.org/10.1097/YCO .0000000000000219.

Harris, Aisha. "A History of Self-Care." Slate, April 5, 2017. http:// www.slate.com/articles/arts/culturebox/2017/04/the_history_of_self_care .html.

Horowitz, Juliana M., and Nikki Graf. "Most U.S. Teens See Anxiety and Depression as a Major Problem among Their Peers." Pew Research Center, February 20, 2019. https://www.pewresearch.org/social-trends/2019/02/20 /most-u-s-teens-see-anxiety-and-depression-as-a-major-problem-among -their-peers/.

Jacobson, Rae. "Should Kids Take Mental Health Days?" Child Mind Institute, September 15, 2022. https://childmind.org/article/should-kids -take-mental-health-days/.

Johns, Michelle M. "Transgender Identity and Experiences of Violence Victimization, Substance Use, Suicide Risk, and Sexual Risk Behaviors among High School Students—19 States and Large Urban School Districts, 2017." *Morbidity and Mortality Weekly Report* 68, no. 3 (January 25, 2019): 67–71. https://www.cdc.gov/mmwr/volumes/68/wr/mm6803a3.htm.

Kann, Laura, Emily O'Malley Olsen, Tim McManus, Steve Kinchen, David Chyen, William A. Harris, Howell Wechsler, and the CDC. "Sexual Identity, Sex of Sexual Contacts, and Health-Risk Behaviors among Students in Grades 9–12—Youth Risk Behavior Surveillance, Selected Sites, United States, 2001–2009." *Morbidity and Mortality Weekly Report* 60, no. 7 (June 2011): 1–133. https://pubmed.ncbi.nlm.nih.gov/21659985/.

Keisler-Starkey, Katherine, and Lisa N. Bunch. "Health Insurance Coverage in the United States: 2020." (Current Population Reports No. P60-274). Washington, DC: United States Census Bureau, September 14, 2021. https://www.census.gov/library/publications/2021/demo/p60-274 .html.

Keller, Sarah, Vanessa McNeill, and Tan Tran. "The Perceived Stigma Reduction Expressed by Young Adults in Response to Suicide Prevention Videos." *International Journal of Environmental Research and Public Health* 18, no. 12 (June 2021): 6180. https://www.ncbi.nlm.nih.gov/pmc/articles /PMC8229221/.

Kelvens, Carissa. "Fear and Anxiety." California State University–Northridge. Accessed March 29, 2022. http://www.csun.edu/~vcpsy00h /students/fear.htm.

Kuzminskaite, Erika, Brenda W. J. H. Penninx, Anne-Laura van Harmelen, Bernet M. Elzinga, Jacqueline G. F. M. Hovens, and Christiaan H. Vinkers. "Childhood Trauma in Adult Depressive and Anxiety Disorders: An Integrated Review on Psychological and Biological Mechanisms in the NESDA Cohort." *Journal of Affective Disorders* 283 (March 2021): 179–191. https://doi.org/10.1016/j.jad.2021.01.054.

Mandell, Wallace. "Origins of Mental Health." Johns Hopkins Bloomberg School of Public Health. Accessed July 21, 2022. https://publichealth.jhu .edu/departments/mental-health/about/origins-of-mental-health.

"Mental Health Disparities: Diverse Populations." American Psychiatric Association. Accessed November 14, 2022. https://www.psychiatry.org /psychiatrists/cultural-competency/education/mental-health-facts.

"Mott Poll Report." *National Poll on Children's Health* 37, no. 15 (January 18, 2021). https://mottpoll.org/reports/teens-talking-teens-about-mental-health.

Negele, Alexa, Johannes Kaufhold, Lisa Kallenbach, and Marianne Leuzinger-Bohleber. "Childhood Trauma and Its Relation to Chronic Depression in Adulthood." *Depression Research and Treatment* (2015). https://doi.org/10.1155/2015/650804.

Oar, Ella L., Carly Johnco, and Thomas H. Ollendick. "Cognitive Behavioral Therapy for Anxiety and Depression in Children and Adolescents." *Psychiatric Clinics of North America* 40, no. 4 (December 2017): 661–674. https://doi.org/10.1016/j.psc.2017.08.002.

Parker, Kim, and Ruth Igielnik. "On the Cusp of Adulthood and Facing an Uncertain Future: What We Know about Gen Z So Far." Pew Research Center, May 14, 2020. https://www.pewresearch.org/social-trends/2020/05/14/on-the-cusp-of-adulthood-and-facing-an-uncertain-future-what-we-know-about-gen-z-so-far.

Pfeiffer, Paul N., Michele Heisler, John D. Piette, Mary A. M. Rogers, and Marcia Valenstein. "Efficacy of Peer Support Interventions for Depression: A Meta-Analysis." *General Hospital Psychiatry* 33, no. 1 (January/February 2011): 29–36. https://doi.org/10.1016/j.genhosppsych.2010.10.002.

"Psychotherapy for Children and Adolescents: Different Types." American Academy of Child and Adolescent Psychiatry, April 2019. https://www.aacap.org/AACAP/Families_and_Youth/Facts_for_Families/FFF-Guide/Psychotherapies-For-Children-And-Adolescents-086.aspx.

Ramachandran, Naman, and Andrew Wallenstein. "Positive On-Screen Mental Health Portrayals Help Teens Discuss Issues, Survey Finds." *Variety*, September 21, 2021. https://variety.com/2021/film/global/teen-mental-health-bbfc-uk-1235069823/.

"Safety Plan." My Safety Plan. Accessed November 14, 2022. https://www.mysafetyplan.org/static/NationalSPA-c4a86b10761e54a2dd835519b48ff479.pdf.

Shelton, Deborah, Karen Kesten, Wanli Zhang, and Robert Trestman. "Impact of a Dialectic Behavior Therapy—Corrections Modified (DBT-CM) upon Behaviorally Challenged Incarcerated Male Adolescents." *Journal of Child and Adolescent Psychiatric Nursing* 24, no. 2 (April 2011): 105–113. https://doi.org/10.1111/j.1744-6171.2011.00275.x.

Simon, Robert I. "Passive Suicidal Ideation: Still a High-Risk Clinical Scenario." *Current Psychology* 13, no. 3 (March 2014): 13–15. Accessed July 21, 2022. https://cdn.mdedge.com/files/s3fs-public/Document/September-2017/013_0314CP_Commentary_FINAL.pdf.

Straub, Joana, Rebecca Brown, Kathrin Malejko, Martina Bonenberger, Georg Grön, Paul L. Piener, and Birgit Abler. "Adolescent Depression and Brain Development: Evidence from Voxel-Based Morphometry." *Journal of Psychiatry & Neuroscience* 44, no. 4 (July 2019): 237–245. https://doi.org/10.1503/jpn.170233.

"Substance Abuse and Mental Health Services Administration. "Key Substance Use and Mental Health Indicators in the United States: Results from the 2020 National Survey on Drug Use and Health." (HHS Publication No. PEP21-07-01-003, NSDUH Series H-56). October 2021. Rockville, MD: Center for Behavioral Health Statistics and Quality, Substance Abuse and Mental Health Services Administration. https://www.samhsa.gov/data/sites/default/files/reports/rpt35325/NSDUHFFRPDFWHTMLFiles2020/2020NSDUHFFR1PDFW102121.pdf.

"Teen Brain: Behavior, Problem Solving, and Decision Making." American Academy of Child and Adolescent Psychiatry, September 2017. https://www.aacap.org/AACAP/Families_and_Youth/Facts_for_Families/FFF-Guide/The-Teen-Brain-Behavior-Problem-Solving-and-Decision-Making-095.aspx.

"Teen Suicide." Johns Hopkins Medicine. Accessed November 14, 2022. https://www.hopkinsmedicine.org/health/conditions-and-diseases/teen-suicide.

"What Are the Five Major Types of Anxiety Disorders?" US Department of Health and Human Services, February 12, 2014. https://www.hhs.gov/answers/mental-health-and-substance-abuse/what-are-the-five-major-types-of-anxiety-disorders/index.html.

"What Is Depression?" Anxiety & Depression Association of America, November 10, 2022. https://adaa.org/understanding-anxiety/depression.

Winerman, Lea. "By the Numbers: Antidepressant Use on the Rise." *Monitor on Psychology* 48, no. 10 (November 2017): 120. https://www.apa.org/monitor/2017/11/numbers.

Yard, Ellen, Lakshmi Radhakrishnan, Michael F. Ballesteros, Michael Sheppard, Abigail Gates, Zachary Stein, Kathleen Hartnett et al. "Emergency Department Visits for Suspected Suicide Attempts among Persons Aged 12–25 Years before and during the COVID-19 Pandemic—United States, January 2019–May 2021." *Morbidity and Mortality Weekly Report* 70, no. 24 (June 18, 2021): 888–894. https://www.cdc.gov/mmwr/volumes/70/wr/mm7024e1.htm.

FURTHER INFORMATION

The Crisis Text Line
https://www.crisistextline.org/
If talking on the phone is a barrier for you, the Crisis Text Line is a 24/7 service that allows you to chat via text messages with someone who can help you in a mental health emergency. Just text HOME to 741741 to get connected. The service's website also provides resources for learning about mental health and opportunities to volunteer.

The Jed Foundation
https://jedfoundation.org/
This mental health resource center is designed for young people and provides the services you need to thrive beyond an immediate crisis. Their menu has two options: I Need Help and I Want to Help. Click on the one that's resonating with you.

Mindfulness for Teens
https://www.mindfulnessforteens.com/
Created by Dr. Dzung Vo, a pediatrician who specializes in adolescent medicine, Mindfulness for Teens provides resources for learning about mindfulness as well as meditations to try. This website is just one of many about mindfulness, so if you're not vibing with the style, check out YouTube or your phone's app store for more meditations. You might even have a meditation center nearby, so try searching "meditation center" in Google Maps if you prefer an in-person experience.

National Alliance on Mental Illness
https://nami.org/
This mental illness advocacy group is dedicated to education, destigmatization, and providing resources. There are also local chapters for you to get involved IRL.

988 Suicide & Crisis Lifeline
https://988lifeline.org/
Dialing or texting 988 on your phone will connect you to the 988 Suicide & Crisis Lifeline, a 24/7 service designed to help you in a mental health crisis or emergency. The lifeline's website also has resources for specific identities you may hold, such as being LGBTQ+ or neurodivergent.

Psychology Today's Find a Therapist Tool
https://www.psychologytoday.com/us/therapists
Many therapists, psychologists, and psychiatrists are listed on this popular publication's website. To find therapists near you and learn about their specialties, enter your zip code in the search bar, or scroll to search by state. Each therapist's profile will tell you what you need to know, including services provided, contact information, credentials, and costs.

The Trevor Project
https://www.thetrevorproject.org/
The Trevor Project is a nonprofit organization working to prevent suicide among LGBTQ+ youth. Their website provides access to counselors with just a click of a button, guides to coming out, and an online community of fellow LGBTQ+ people aged thirteen to twenty-four from all over the globe. If you need to, you can close the site quickly with a handy shortcut: hit the Esc key on your keyboard three times.

Understood.org
https://www.understood.org/
This resource is for neurodivergent young people meant to help them find resources, community, and strategies for accepting and celebrating their differences.

INDEX

ABOUT THE AUTHOR

Katherine (Katie) Speller is a Hudson Valley, New York–based writer and editor who should probably consider inserting a third thing here someday. After studying journalism at SUNY New Paltz, she's spent most of her career telling stories that break her heart and put it back together again in equal measure, and the rest of it making mediocre jokes. She's had the honor of being a storyteller, advocate, mentor, and friend to countless communities of teen readers over the years through her work at MTV News, Bustle, Her Campus, and more. Her coverage of politics, social issues, and culture have been published in many magazines and news sites, including *Women's Health*, *Bitch*, the Daily Dot, WNYC, and Public Radio International (PRI). A Libra, a tarot reader, and a tattoo collector, she firmly believes in the healing powers of Stephen Sondheim, regional gas station chain coffee, and committing to the bit.

ABOUT THE ILLUSTRATOR

Harshad Marathe is an illustrator and storyteller. He has an MFA from the School of Visual Arts in New York City and has illustrated many books. He has backpacked all over the world.